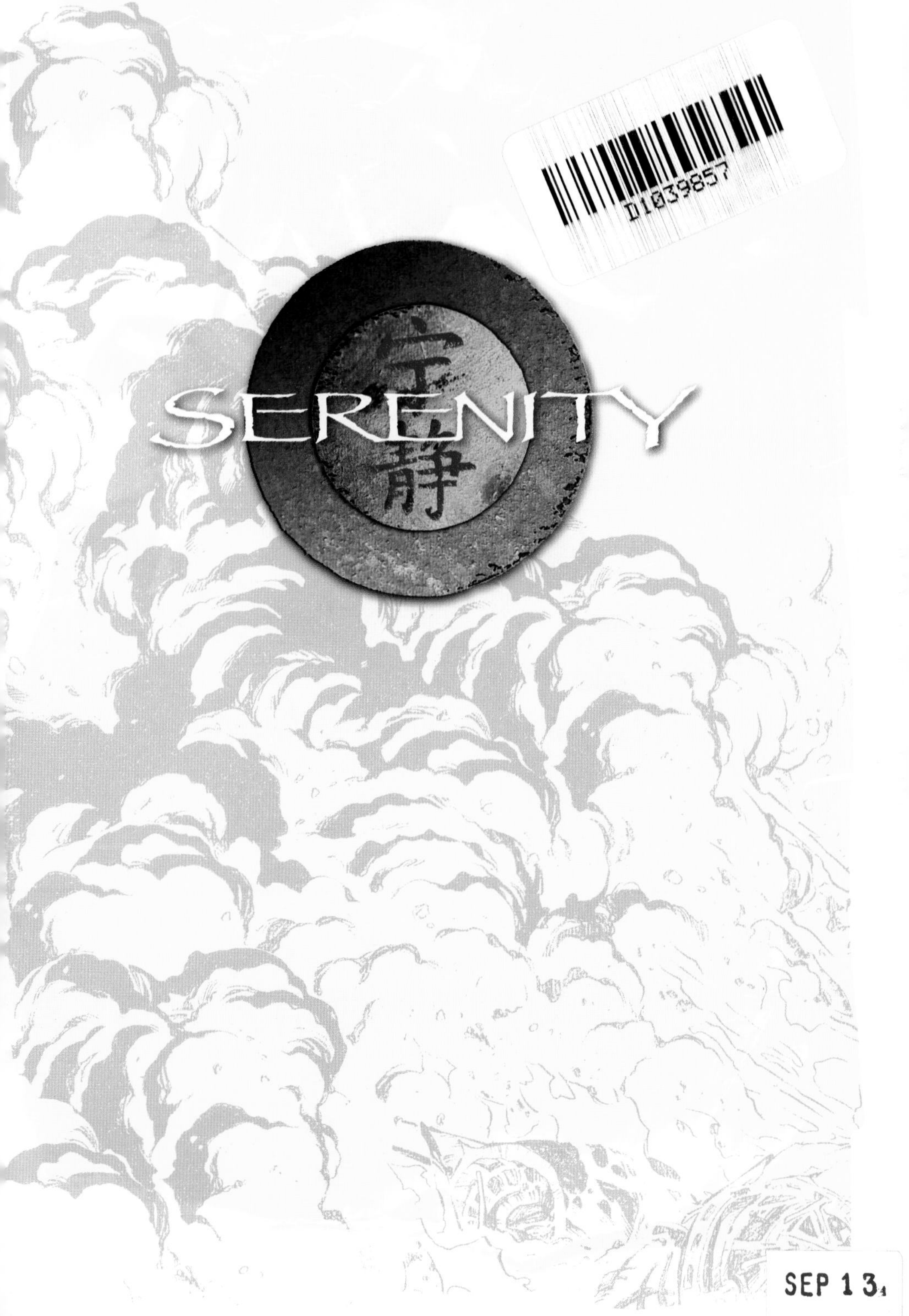
SERENITY
宁静

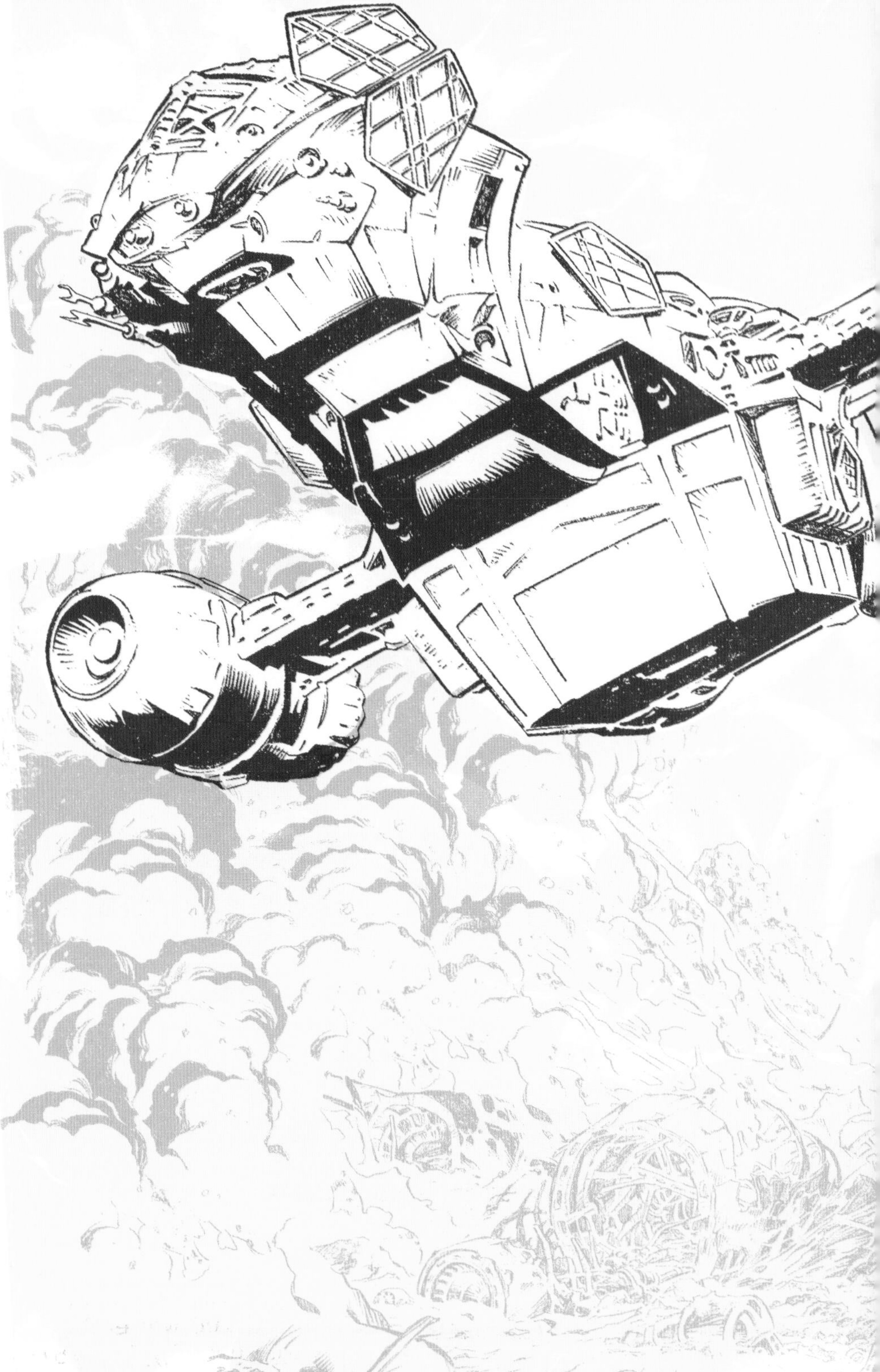

BETTER DAYS

SCRIPT BY **Joss Whedon and Brett Matthews**
ART BY **Will Conrad**
COLORS BY **Michelle Madsen**
LETTERS BY **Michael Heisler**
COVER BY **Jo Chen**
ORIGINAL SERIES COVERS BY **Adam Hughes**

Dark Horse Books®

Publisher **Mike Richardson**
Editor **Scott Allie**
Associate Editor **Sierra Hahn**
Collection Designers **Scott Cook and Heidi Whitcomb**
Art Director **Lia Ribacchi**

Special thanks to Cindy Chang at Universal Studios.
Special thanks also to Michael Boretz, Julia Dalzell, Natalie Farrell, J. P. Bernardo,
Debbie Olshan, Deborah Hsu, and Han Way Lee.

帶勁

Published by
Dark Horse Books
A division of
Dark Horse Comics, Inc.
10956 SE Main Street
Milwaukie OR 97222

darkhorse.com

To find a comics shop in your area, call the Comic Shop Locator Service toll-free at 1-888-266-4226

First edition: October 2008
ISBN: 978-1-59582-162-1

5 7 9 10 8 6 4

Printed at Midas Printing International, Ltd., Huizhou, China

This volume collects issues one through three of the Dark Horse comic-book series *Serenity: Better Days*.

A Note to Parents: *Serenity* is rated PG-13. Consult www.filmratings.com for further information.

INTRODUCTION

When Joss Whedon gave me the chance to play a man called Jayne, the "Hero of Canton," I couldn't believe my luck. I'd never been asked to play a girl before, so I knew I was going to have to summon my inner hero, Carol Burnett.

Joss's way with words provided me the opportunity to play a tough guy (girl's name) with comedic flair. In the past, I had been typically cast in roles that called on me to be tough, so to be tough and funny was a great adventure.

In 2002, the script for *Firefly* landed on my doorstep. This was the start of my days as a conduit for those mind-bending Whedonisms. The characters not only cussed in Chinese, they were also fluent in sarcasm. Not only did I fall in love with Jayne's sense of humor, but the show brought endless laughter, banter, practical jokes, and lifelong friendships as a bonus.

Fans' thoughtful and detailed examinations of all areas of *Firefly*, along with their kindness and encouragement, lifted our spirits and reinforced our dedication to delivering what we thought was the best danged show on television. *Firefly* had the most fun writing, hardest-working professional crew, and dedicated support staff I'd ever seen. We were all honored and blessed to be a part of such an amazing team.

So, when it was announced to the cast and crew of *Firefly* on that cold December night that the network was pulling the plug, we all felt as if we were being disemboweled by Reavers. The show had been a blessing and a beacon of light in the lives of all involved, and we felt a great sense of loss that night. Yay, Mudders' Milk! (the perfect disinfectant for Reaver-disembowelment).

Then came an unprecedented Hollywood story of redemption and renewal . . .

Joss called to tell us that he would find a way to keep Serenity flying, even if he had to erect the sets in his backyard (which isn't quite big enough for a spaceship . . . and construction permits are really complicated in his neighborhood). This is not something we soldiers of Hollywood ever hear. When Joss realized that he was producing a new project, I think he came to the conclusion that he was going to need his backyard for his kids, so off he went in search of another hangar for the ship and its crew.

Universal to the rescue!

Before we knew it, we got the shiniest news. We were going to be flying to the outer planets by summer, and not for television, but in a major-motion-picture release by Universal Studios. Joss had done it. He was able to take an old broken-down craft and splintered crew, persuade the Hollywood powers that be to patch up the ship and crew, and get us back in the air. After many months of blogging with fans of undying passion, Joss was getting to bring his crew to the big screen. He had fought the toughest battle, and he had won.

Fearlessly led back out into the Black by Joss, we shared in your hopes that Serenity would fly even higher than before.

It was summer of 2004 in Los Angeles, and we were at home again, this time on the Universal lot. The sets were bigger and badder than I could remember during the series: life was grand. Somewhere near the end of the shoot the cast boarded a more modern craft and took the short trek to Comic-Con in San Diego. As the trailer for the movie played to an unprecedented crowd of nearly 6,000 fans, every hair on my neck was standing. Joss and the fans had gotten their well-deserved wish. They were going to get their movie. I was joyous for *Firefly*'s beloved fans, and even more so for Joss. He'd done the impossible.

What an incredible feat. *Dare to dream*, I thought at that moment. And then: *Wow, who is this Joss guy anyway? How does he create such magic? Where did these people come from? How lucky am I to have had the opportunity to live in this wonderful world of Whedon?*

Now with the Dark Horse comic series of *Serenity*, we all have more chances to devour the characters Joss brought to life when Serenity took its maiden voyage.

I have been very blessed to be forever known as "The-Man-They-Call-Jayne," Gorrammit!

—ADAM BALDWIN
(not a girl's name)

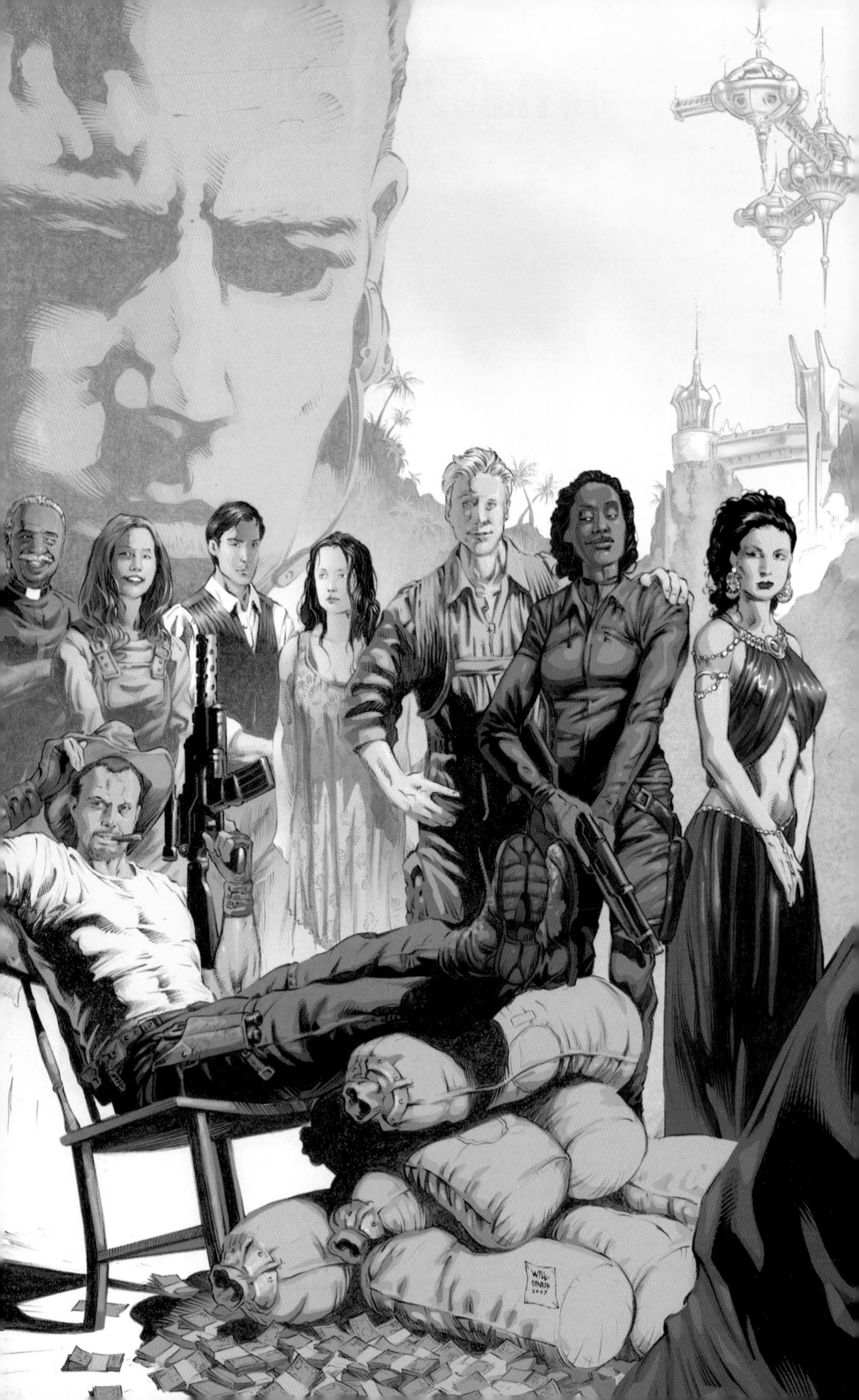
WILL CONRAD 2007

AFTER THE EARTH WAS USED UP, we found a new solar system, and hundreds of new Earths were terra-formed and colonized. The central planets formed the Alliance and decided all the planets had to join under their rule. There was some disagreement on that point. After the War, many of the Independents who had fought and lost drifted to the edges of the system, far from Alliance control. Out here, people struggled to get by with the most basic technologies; a ship would bring you work, a gun would help you keep it. A captain's goal was simple: find a crew, find a job, keep flying.

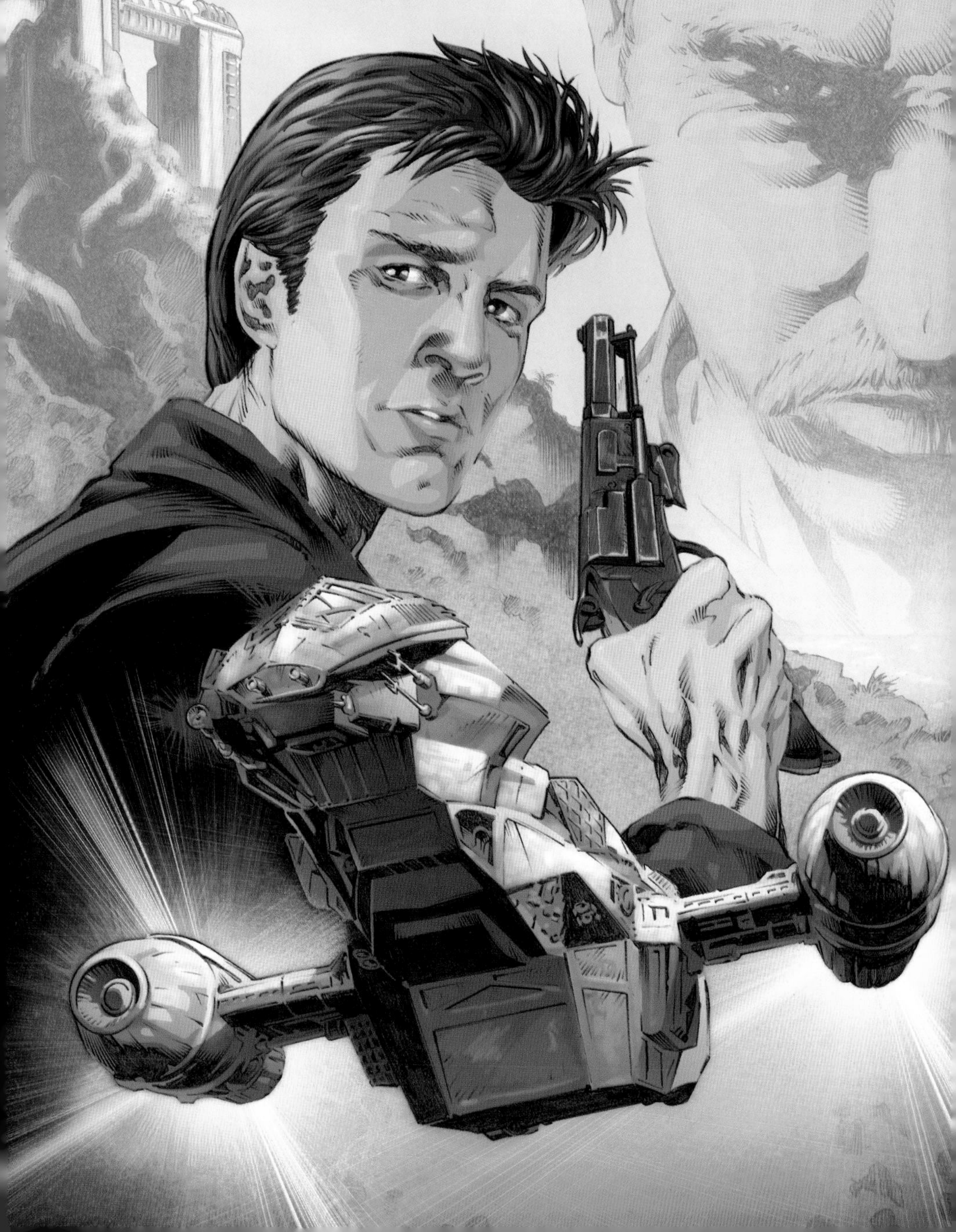

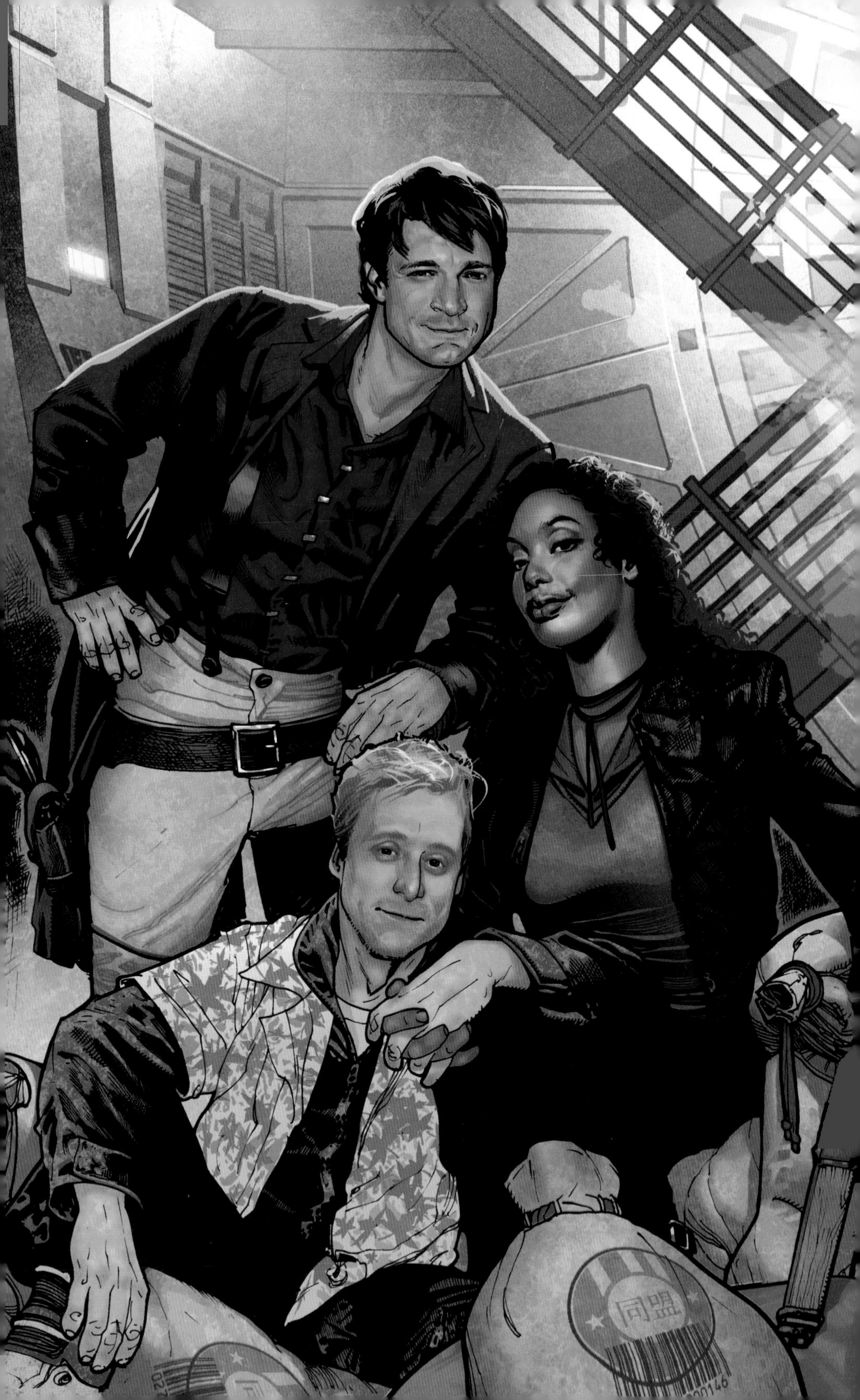
同盟

I DON'T LIKE SPEECHES.

AND UNLIKE MOST WHO SAY THAT, I'M NOT GOING TO FOLLOW BY GIVING ONE.

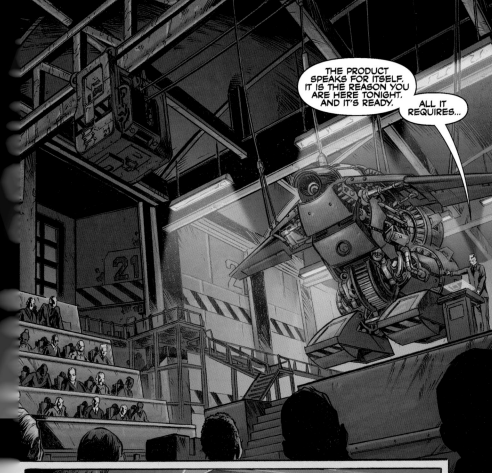

THE PRODUCT SPEAKS FOR ITSELF. IT IS THE REASON YOU ARE HERE TONIGHT, AND IT'S READY.

ALL IT REQUIRES...

...IS SOMEONE STUPID ENOUGH TO ATTRACT ITS ATTENTION.

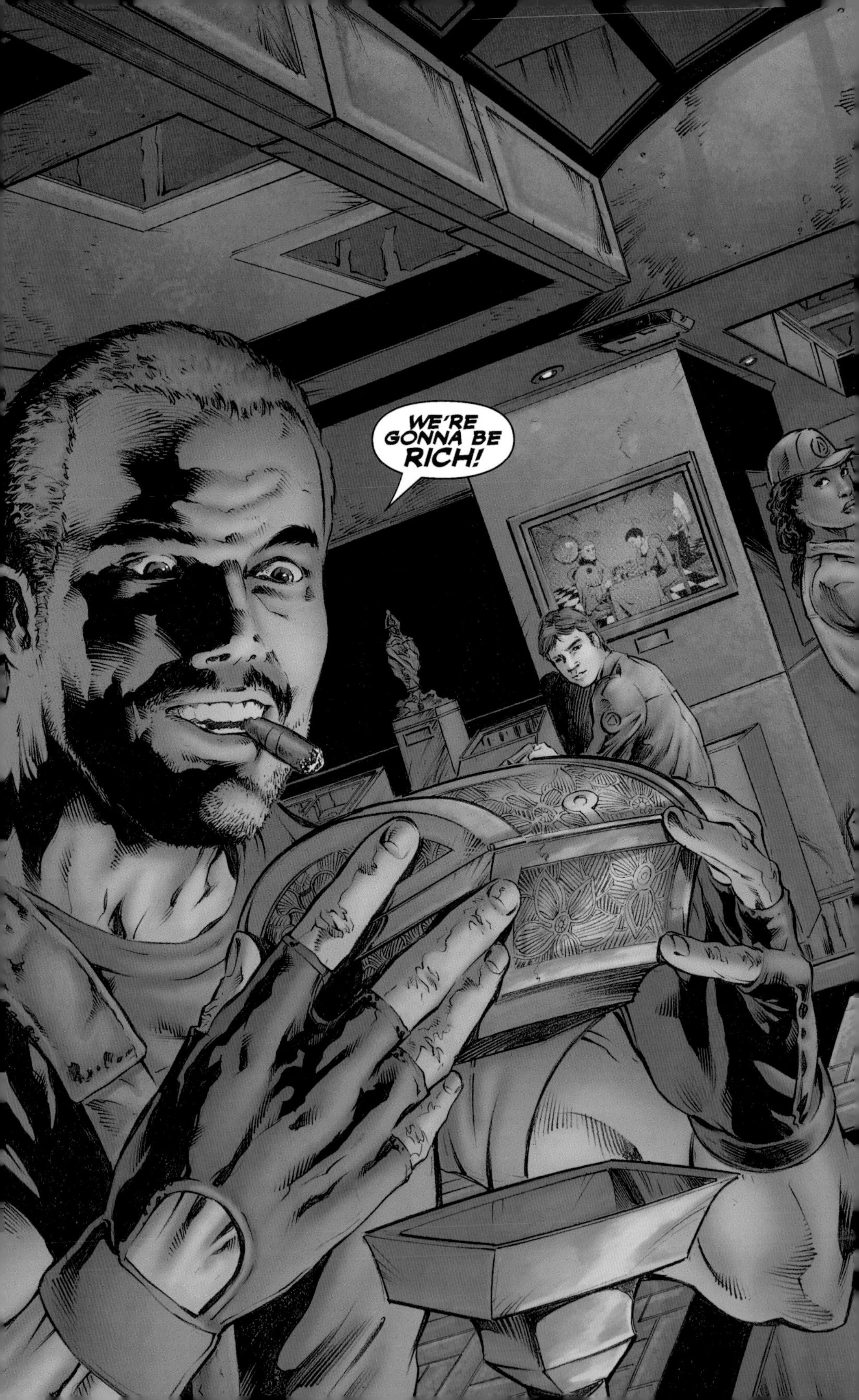
WE'RE GONNA BE RICH!

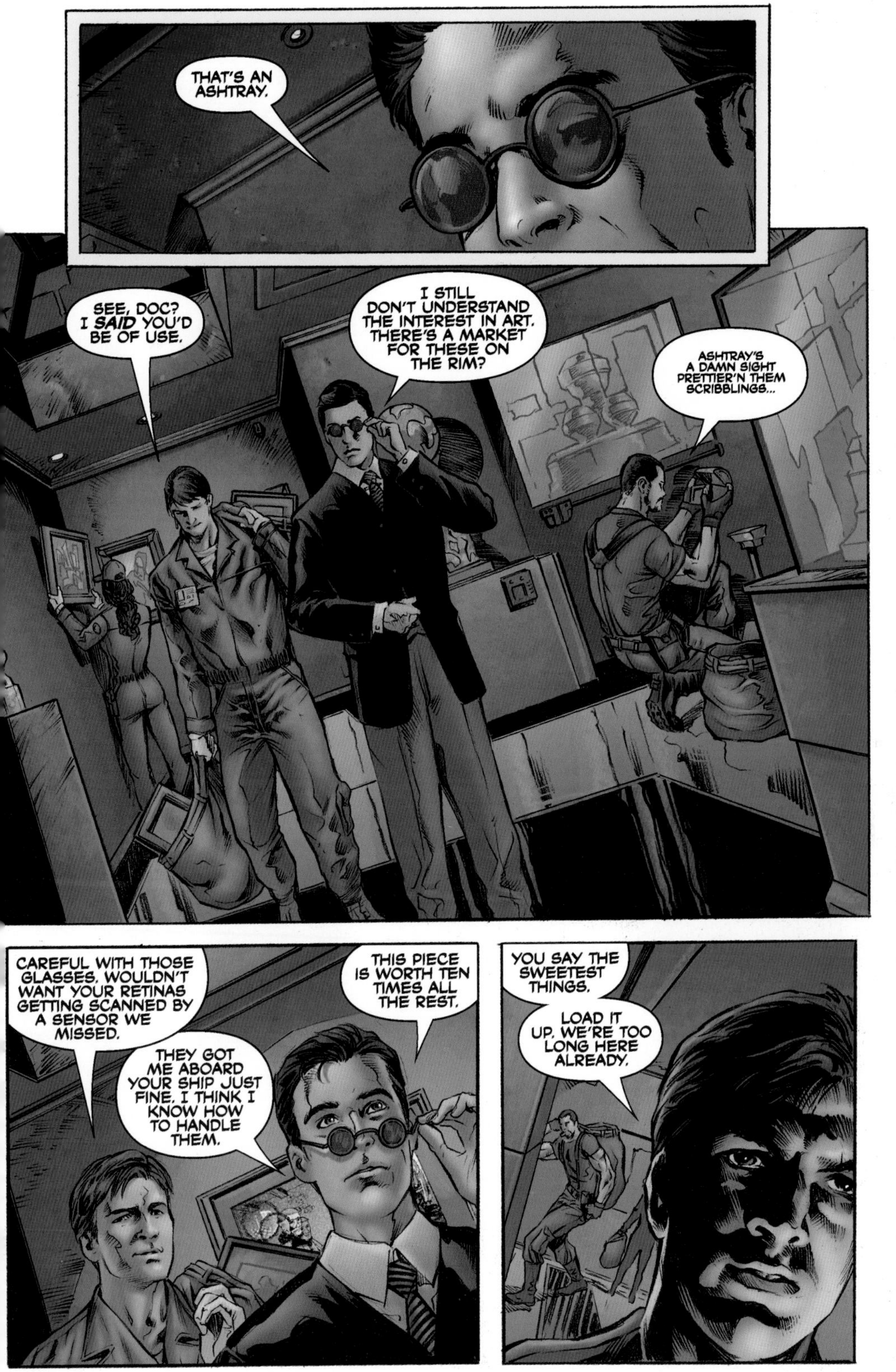
THAT'S AN ASHTRAY.
SEE, DOC? I SAID YOU'D BE OF USE.
I STILL DON'T UNDERSTAND THE INTEREST IN ART. THERE'S A MARKET FOR THESE ON THE RIM?
ASHTRAY'S A DAMN SIGHT PRETTIER'N THEM SCRIBBLINGS...
CAREFUL WITH THOSE GLASSES. WOULDN'T WANT YOUR RETINAS GETTING SCANNED BY A SENSOR WE MISSED.
THEY GOT ME ABOARD YOUR SHIP JUST FINE. I THINK I KNOW HOW TO HANDLE THEM.
THIS PIECE IS WORTH TEN TIMES ALL THE REST.
YOU SAY THE SWEETEST THINGS.
LOAD IT UP, WE'RE TOO LONG HERE ALREADY.

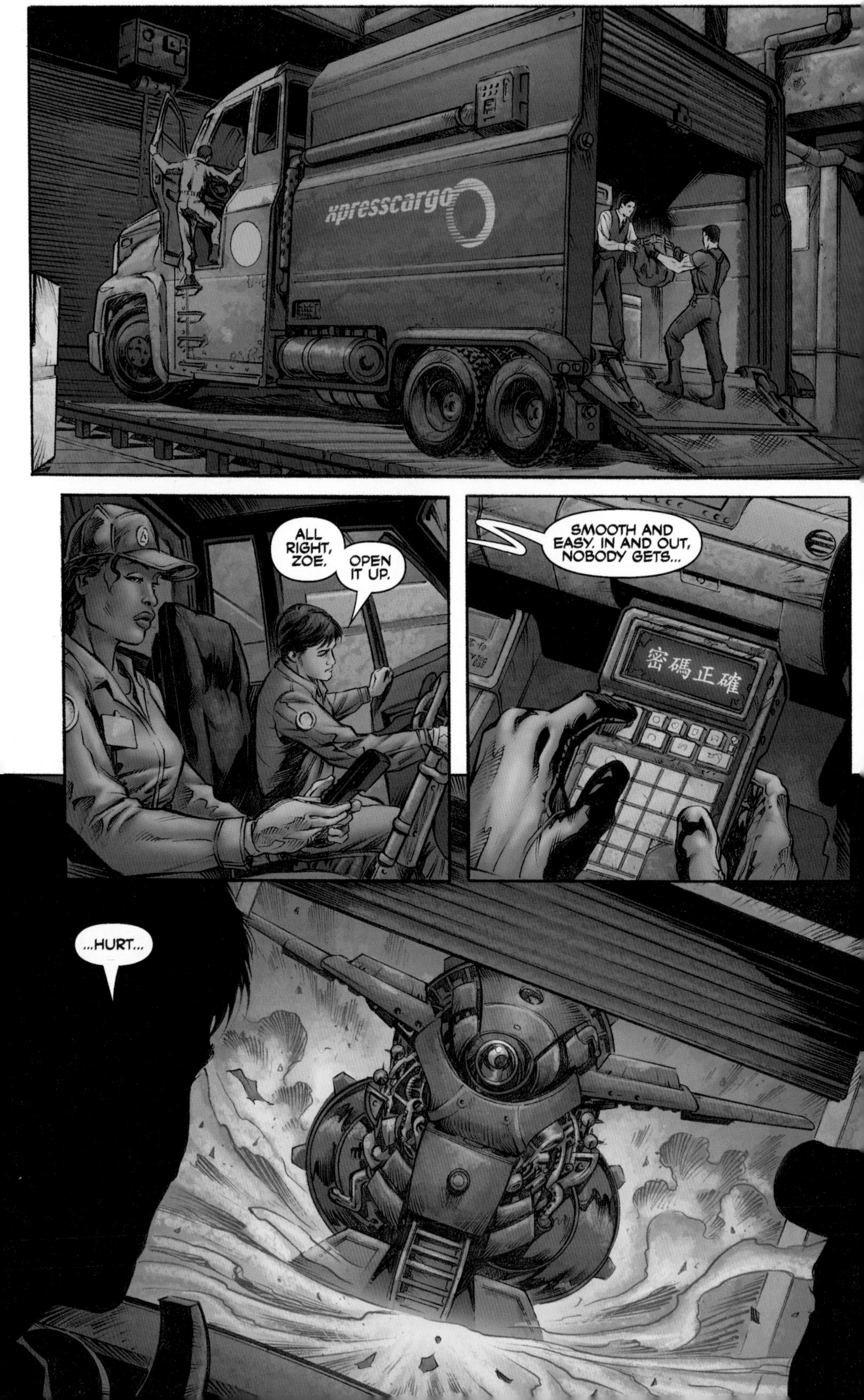
xpresscargo
ALL RIGHT, ZOE.
OPEN IT UP.
SMOOTH AND EASY. IN AND OUT, NOBODY GETS...
密碼正確
...HURT...

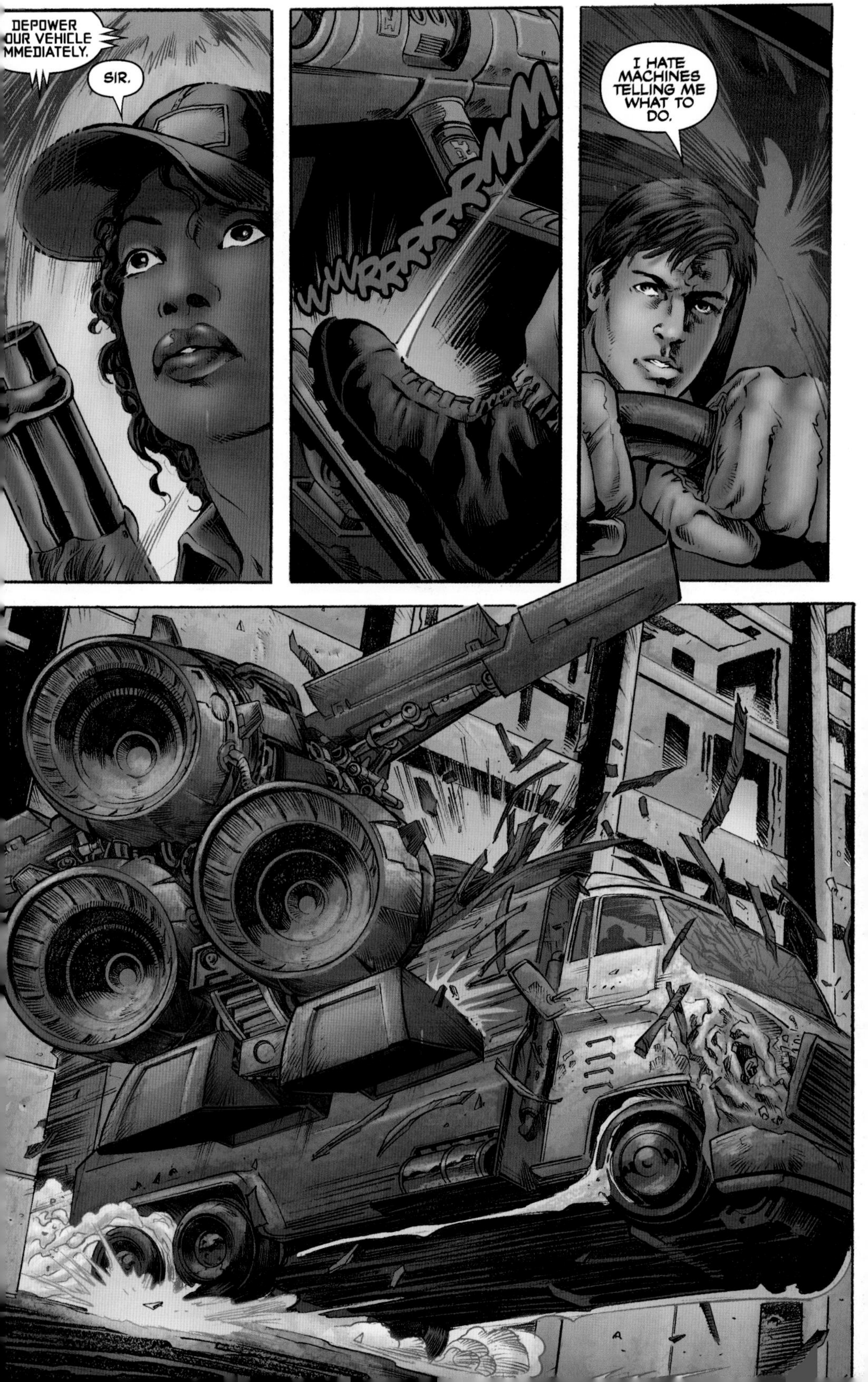
DEPOWER
OUR VEHICLE
MMEDIATELY.
SIR.
WWRRRRRMM
I HATE MACHINES TELLING ME WHAT TO DO.

VROOM

IT'S CHASING US.

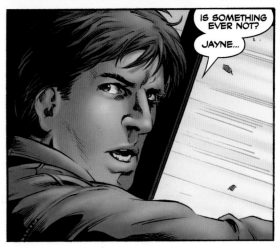

IS SOMETHING EVER NOT?

JAYNE...

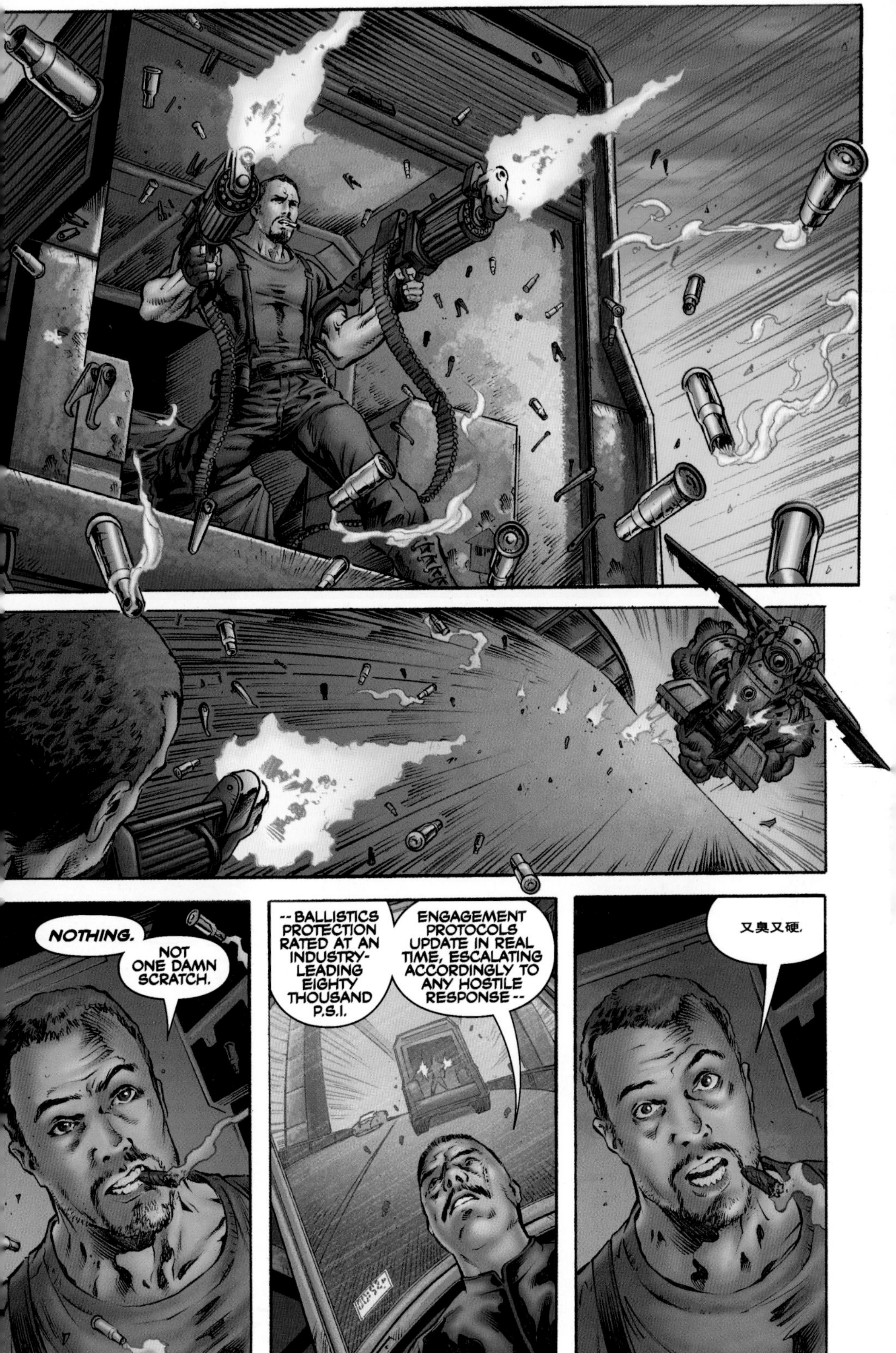
NOTHING.
NOT ONE DAMN SCRATCH.
-- BALLISTICS PROTECTION RATED AT AN INDUSTRY-LEADING EIGHTY THOUSAND P.S.I.
ENGAGEMENT PROTOCOLS UPDATE IN REAL TIME, ESCALATING ACCORDINGLY TO ANY HOSTILE RESPONSE --
又臭又硬,

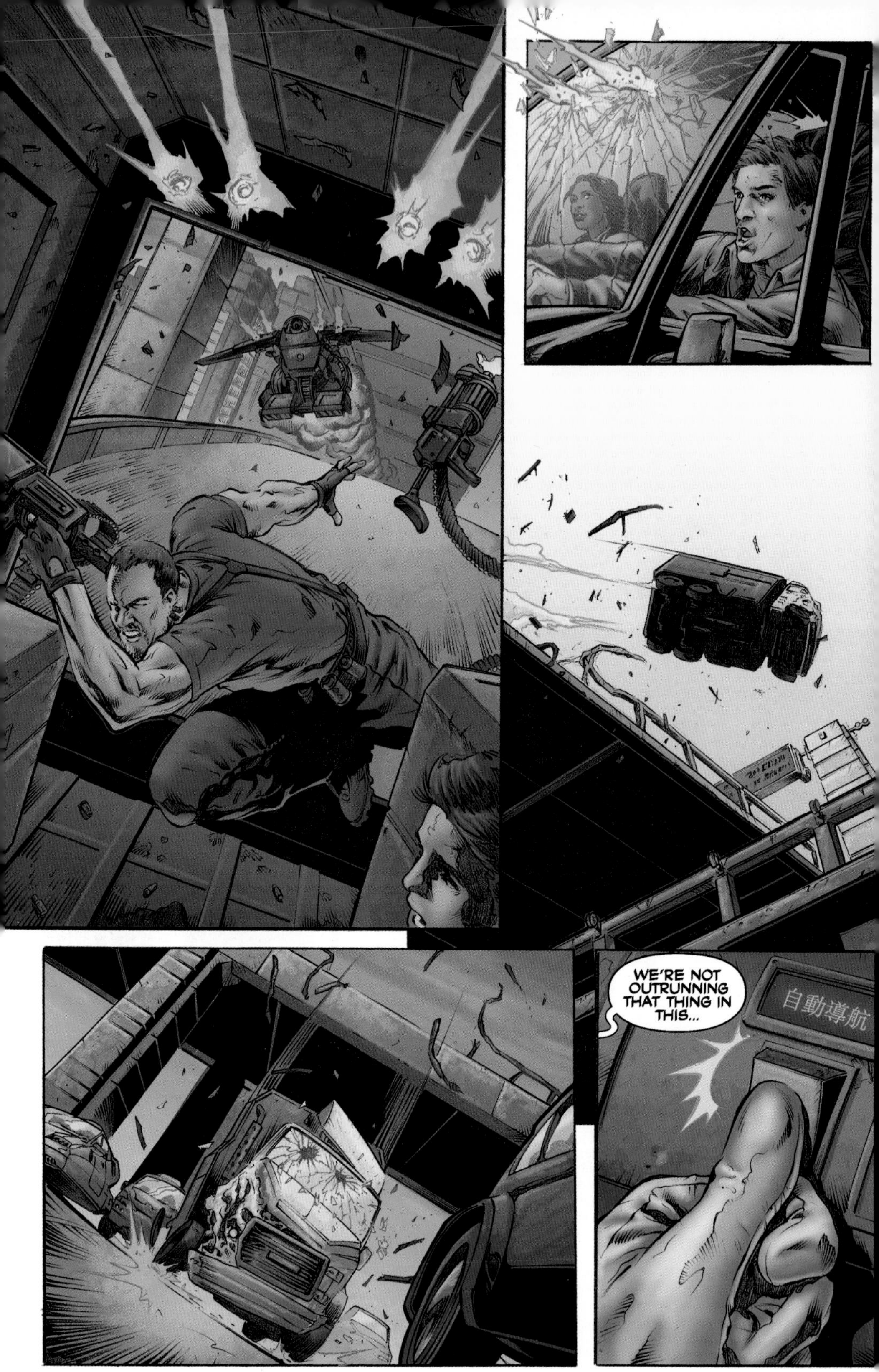
WE'RE NOT OUTRUNNING THAT THING IN THIS...
自動導航

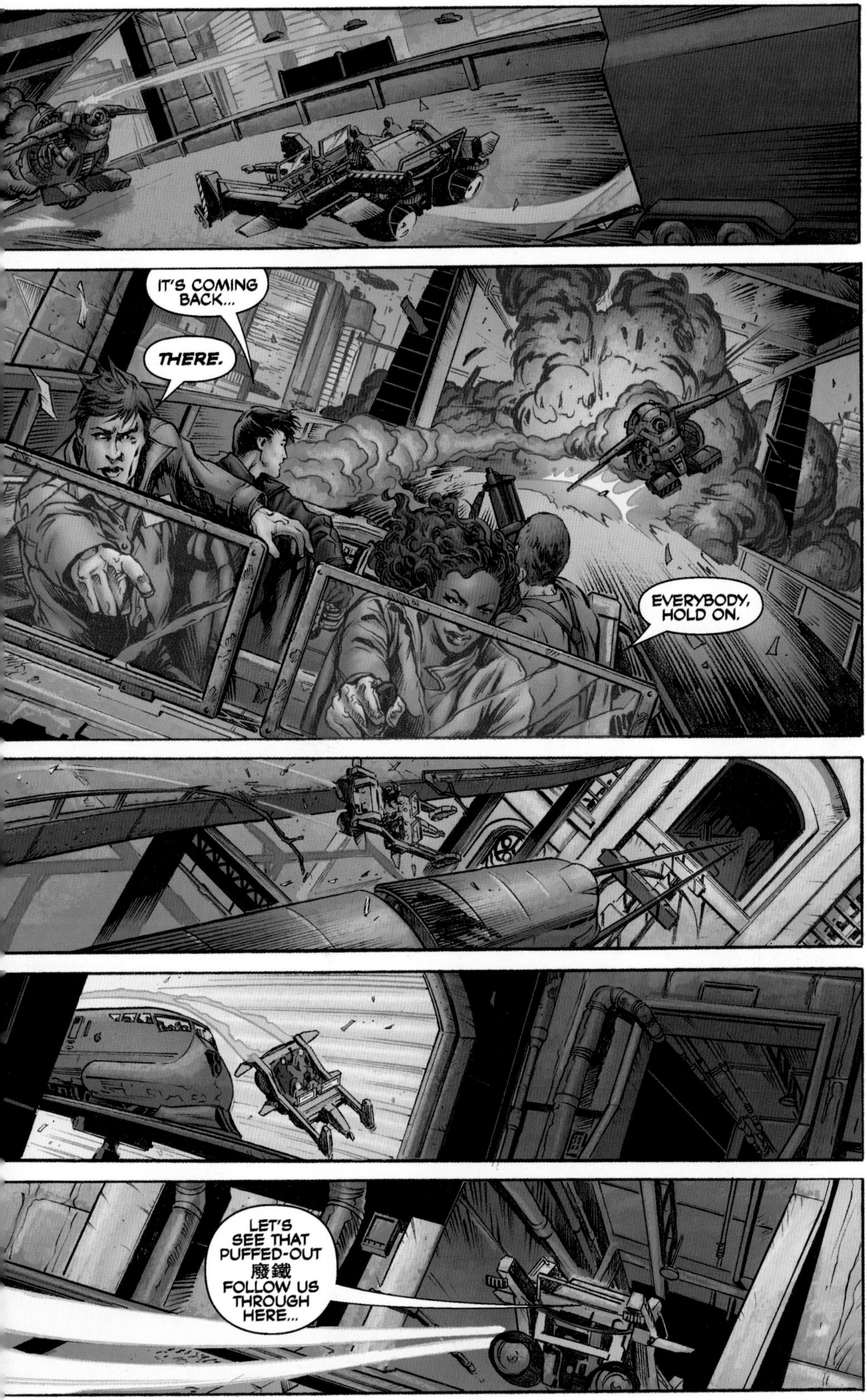
IT'S COMING BACK...
THERE.
EVERYBODY, HOLD ON.
LET'S SEE THAT PUFFED-OUT 廢鐵 FOLLOW US THROUGH HERE...

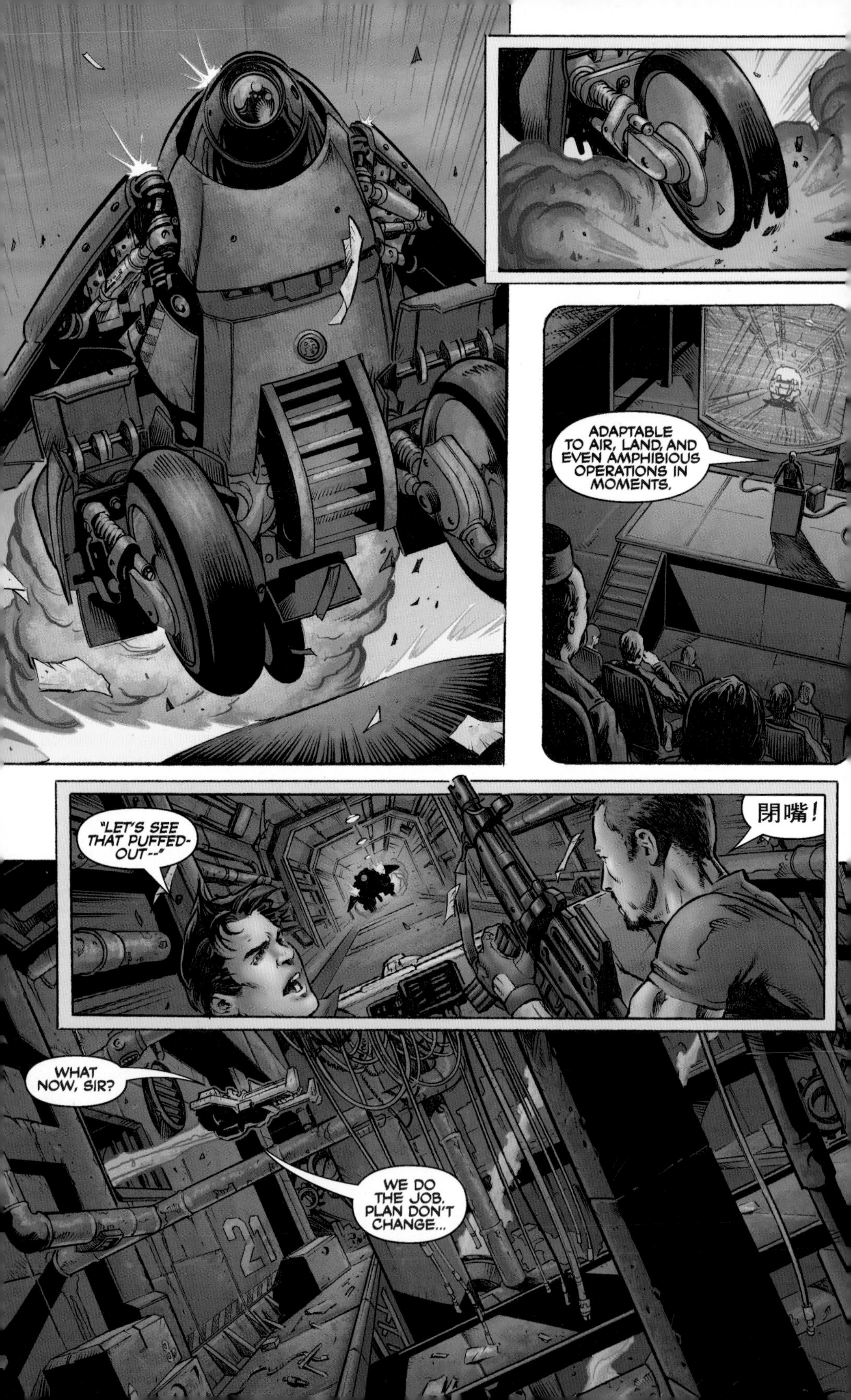
ADAPTABLE TO AIR, LAND, AND EVEN AMPHIBIOUS OPERATIONS IN MOMENTS.
"LET'S SEE THAT PUFFED-OUT--"
閉嘴!
WHAT NOW, SIR?
WE DO THE JOB. PLAN DON'T CHANGE...

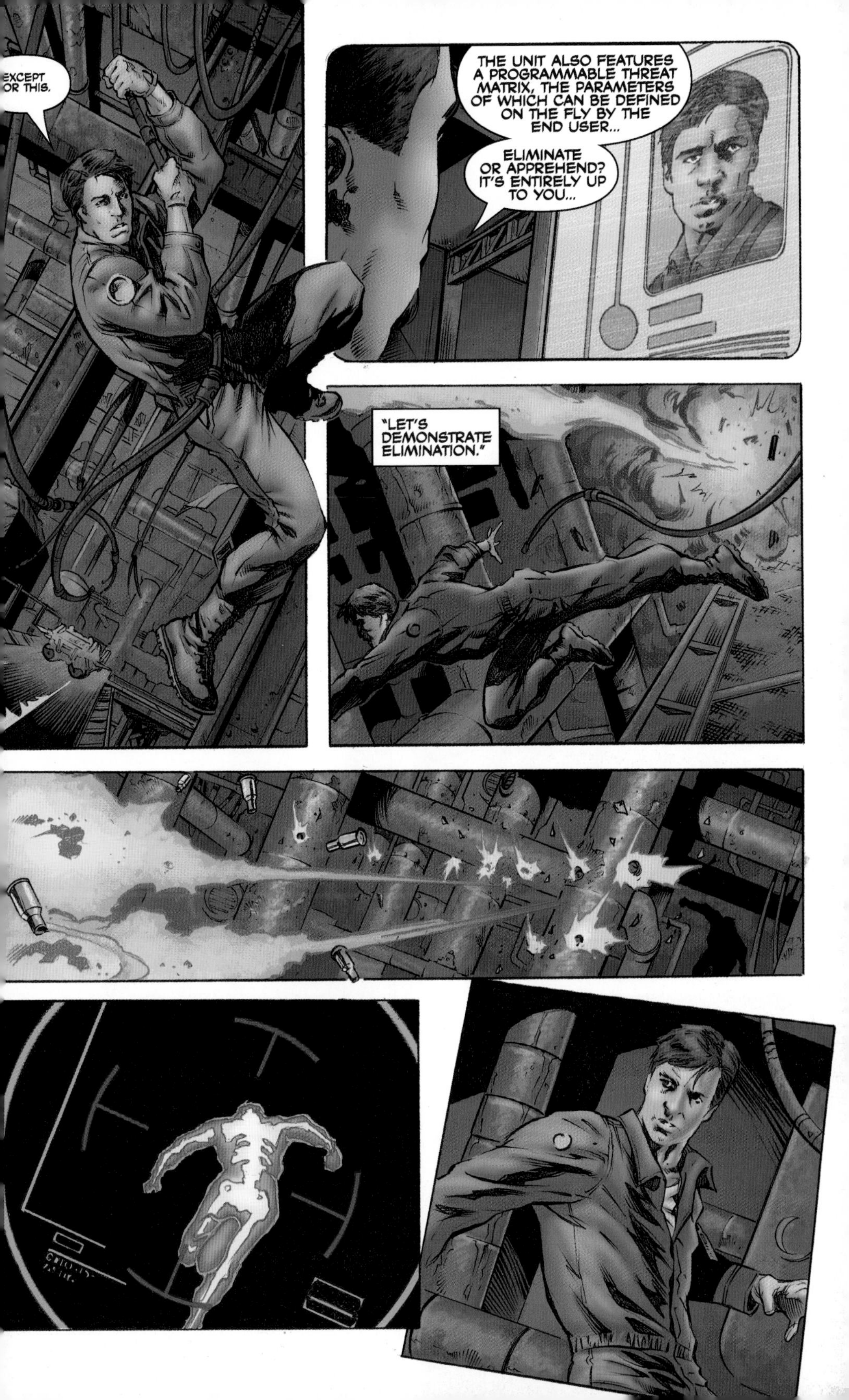
EXCEPT
OR THIS.
THE UNIT ALSO FEATURES A PROGRAMMABLE THREAT MATRIX, THE PARAMETERS OF WHICH CAN BE DEFINED ON THE FLY BY THE END USER...
ELIMINATE OR APPREHEND? IT'S ENTIRELY UP TO YOU...
"LET'S DEMONSTRATE ELIMINATION."

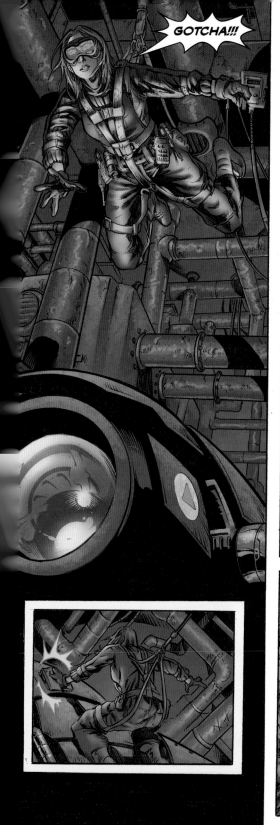

GOTCHA!!!

JEEPERS, CAP'N. DID YOU REALLY HAFTA--

I REALLY DID.

YOU MADE IT.

DON'T SOUND SO DISAPPOINTED, JAYNE.

GIVE KAYLEE A HAND GETTING IT TIED DOWN, AND BE CAREFUL. THING'S WORTH MORE THAN ALL OF US PUT TOGETHER.

WE GOT A DELIVERY TO MAKE.

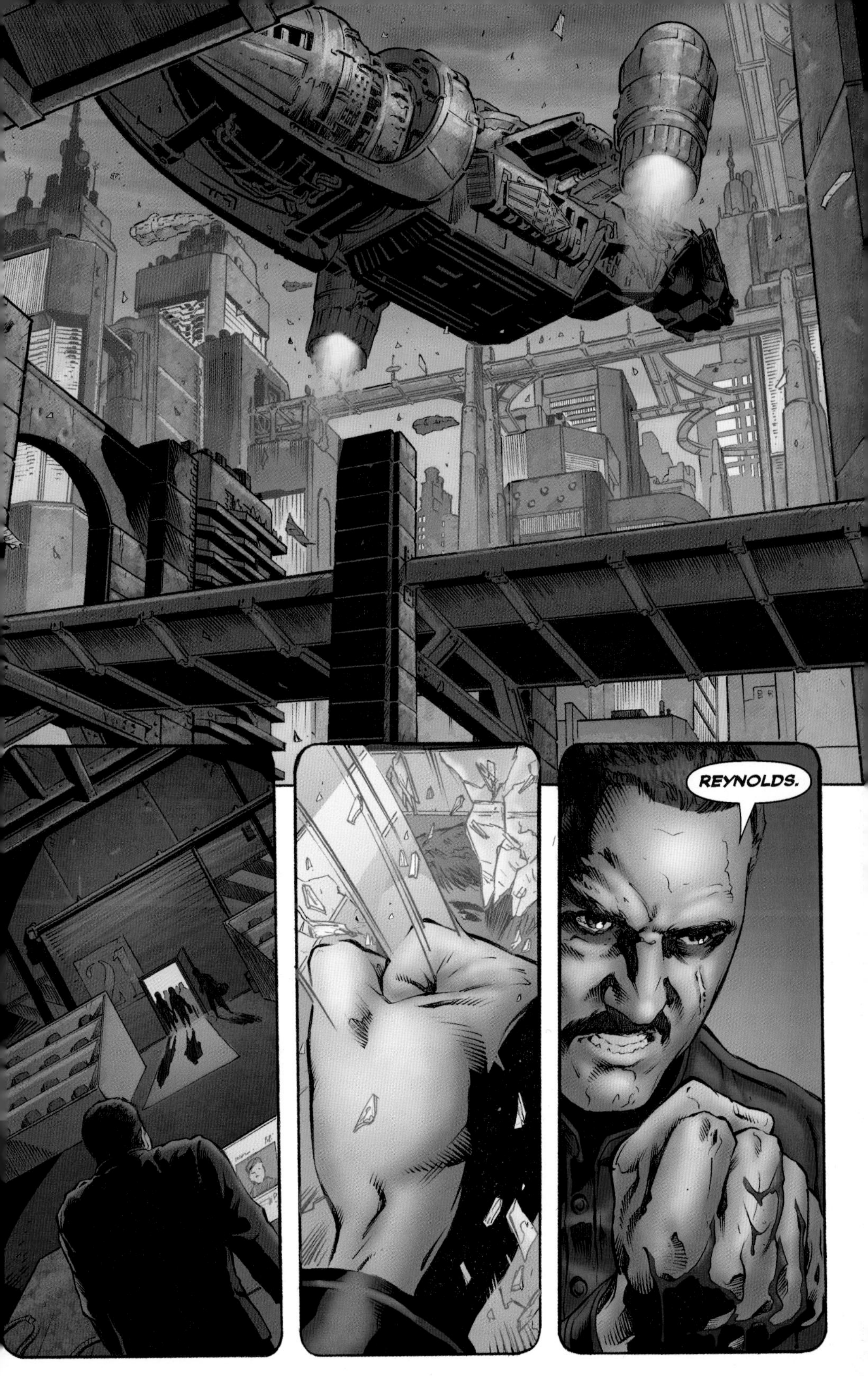
REYNOLDS.

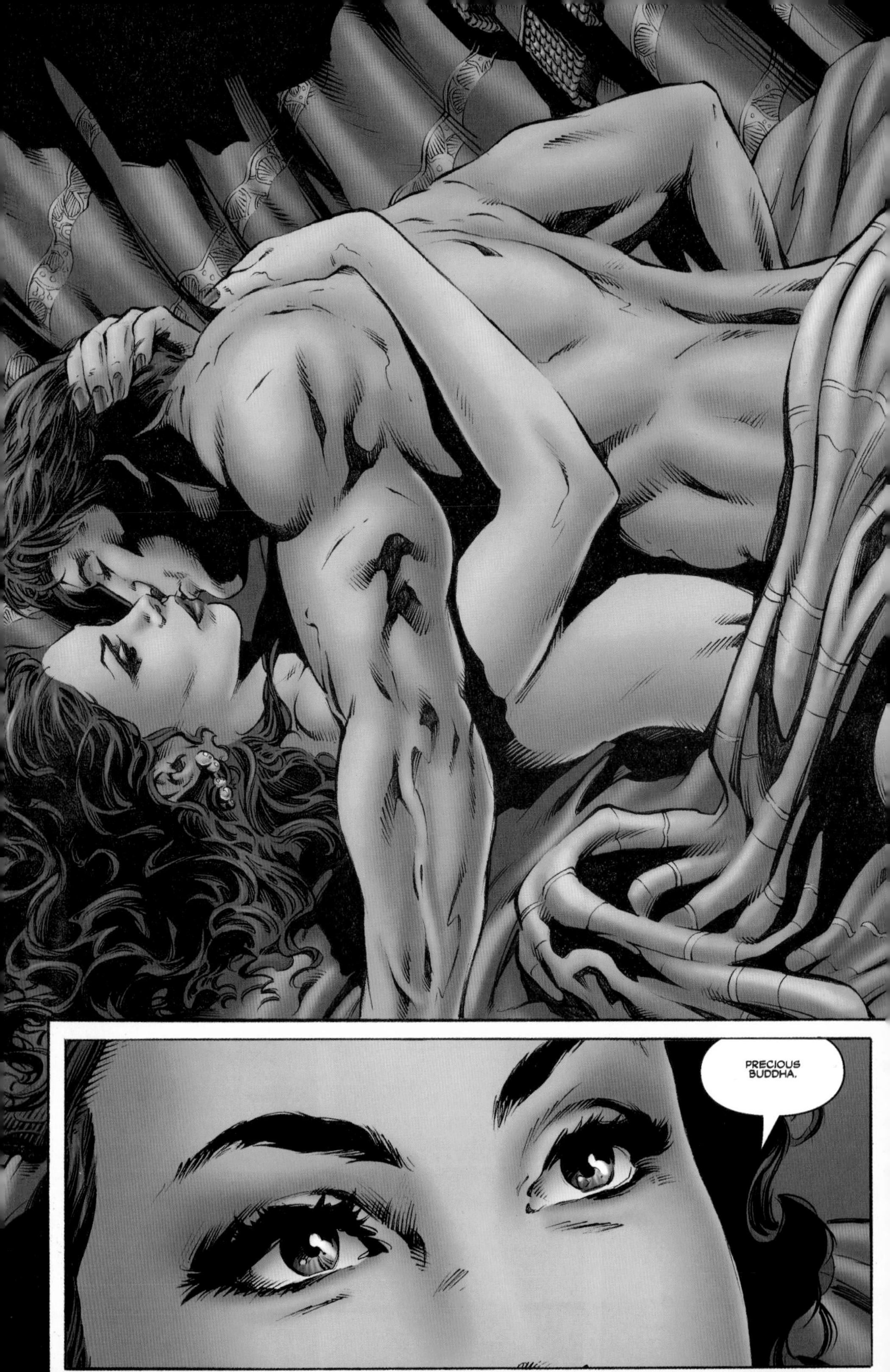
PRECIOUS BUDDHA.

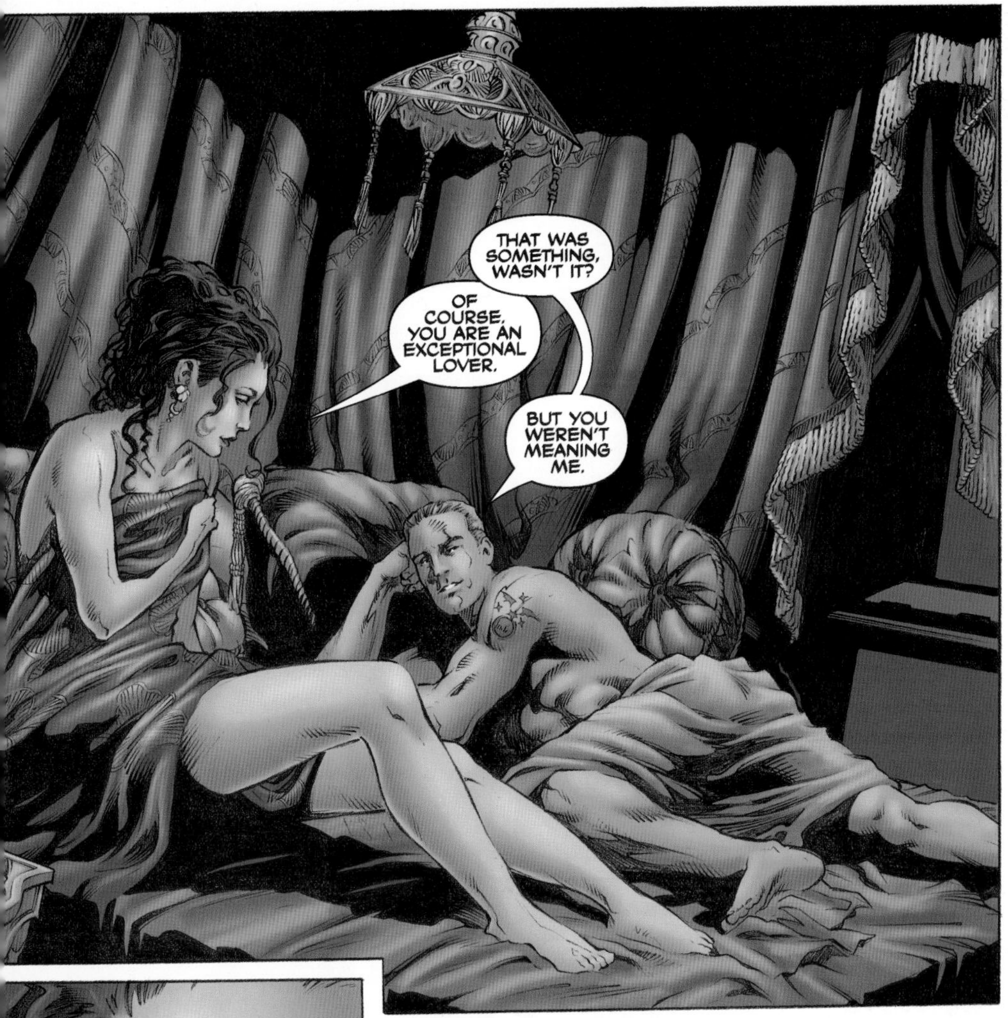
THAT WAS SOMETHING, WASN'T IT?
OF COURSE, YOU ARE AN EXCEPTIONAL LOVER.
BUT YOU WEREN'T MEANING ME.

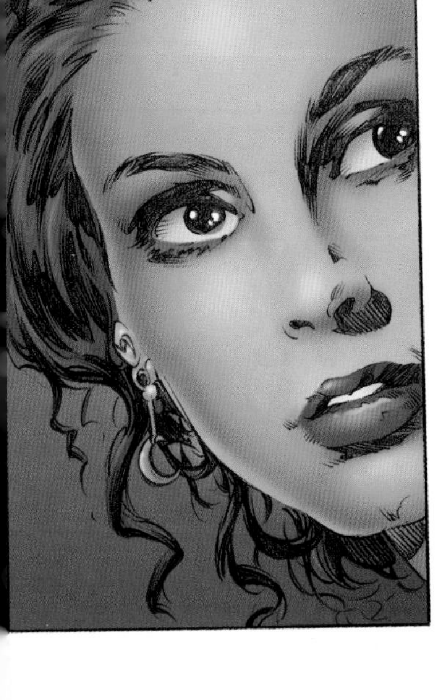

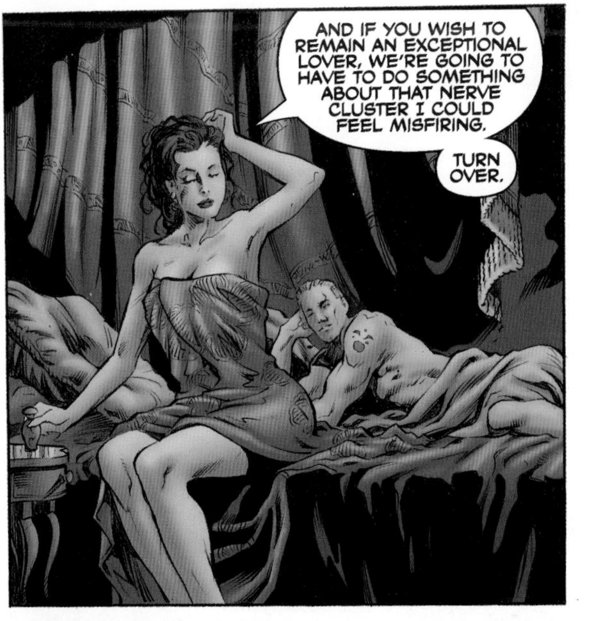
AND IF YOU WISH TO REMAIN AN EXCEPTIONAL LOVER, WE'RE GOING TO HAVE TO DO SOMETHING ABOUT THAT NERVE CLUSTER I COULD FEEL MISFIRING.
TURN OVER.

I DON'T HOLD IT AGAINST YOU.

BEST NOT TO DWELL ON AN OLD SOLDIER LIKE ME. OR HIS WOUNDS.

THERE'S MUCH MORE TO YOU THAN THAT, EPHRAIM.

AND AS I EXPECTED, YOU'RE COMPLETELY OUT OF ALIGNMENT.

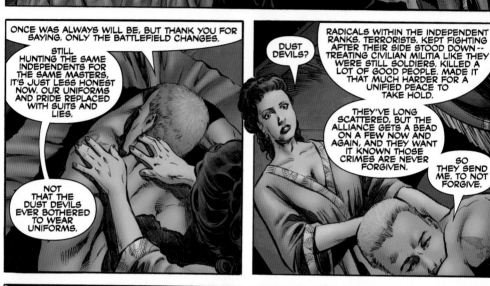

ONCE WAS ALWAYS WILL BE, BUT THANK YOU FOR SAYING. ONLY THE BATTLEFIELD CHANGES.

STILL HUNTING THE SAME INDEPENDENTS FOR THE SAME MASTERS, IT'S JUST LESS HONEST NOW. OUR UNIFORMS AND PRIDE REPLACED WITH SUITS AND LIES.

NOT THAT THE DUST DEVILS EVER BOTHERED TO WEAR UNIFORMS.

DUST DEVILS?

RADICALS WITHIN THE INDEPENDENT RANKS. TERRORISTS, KEPT FIGHTING AFTER THEIR SIDE STOOD DOWN -- TREATING CIVILIAN MILITIA LIKE THEY WERE STILL SOLDIERS. KILLED A LOT OF GOOD PEOPLE. MADE IT THAT MUCH HARDER FOR A UNIFIED PEACE TO TAKE HOLD.

THEY'VE LONG SCATTERED, BUT THE ALLIANCE GETS A BEAD ON A FEW NOW AND AGAIN, AND THEY WANT IT KNOWN THOSE CRIMES ARE NEVER FORGIVEN.

SO THEY SEND ME. TO NOT FORGIVE.

I'M SURPRISED YOU DON'T KNOW THE TERM. "DUST DEVILS" IS SPOKEN WITH PRIDE OUT HERE ON THE RIM. LOCAL HEROES TO SOME FOOLS. YOU KNOW THE TYPE:

HEADSTRONG, SUSPICIOUS, USUALLY SOME KIND OF PETTY THIEF --

KKRAKK

THANKS FOR THE ADJUSTMENT. I FEEL A WORLD BETTER ALREADY.

ANYTIME.

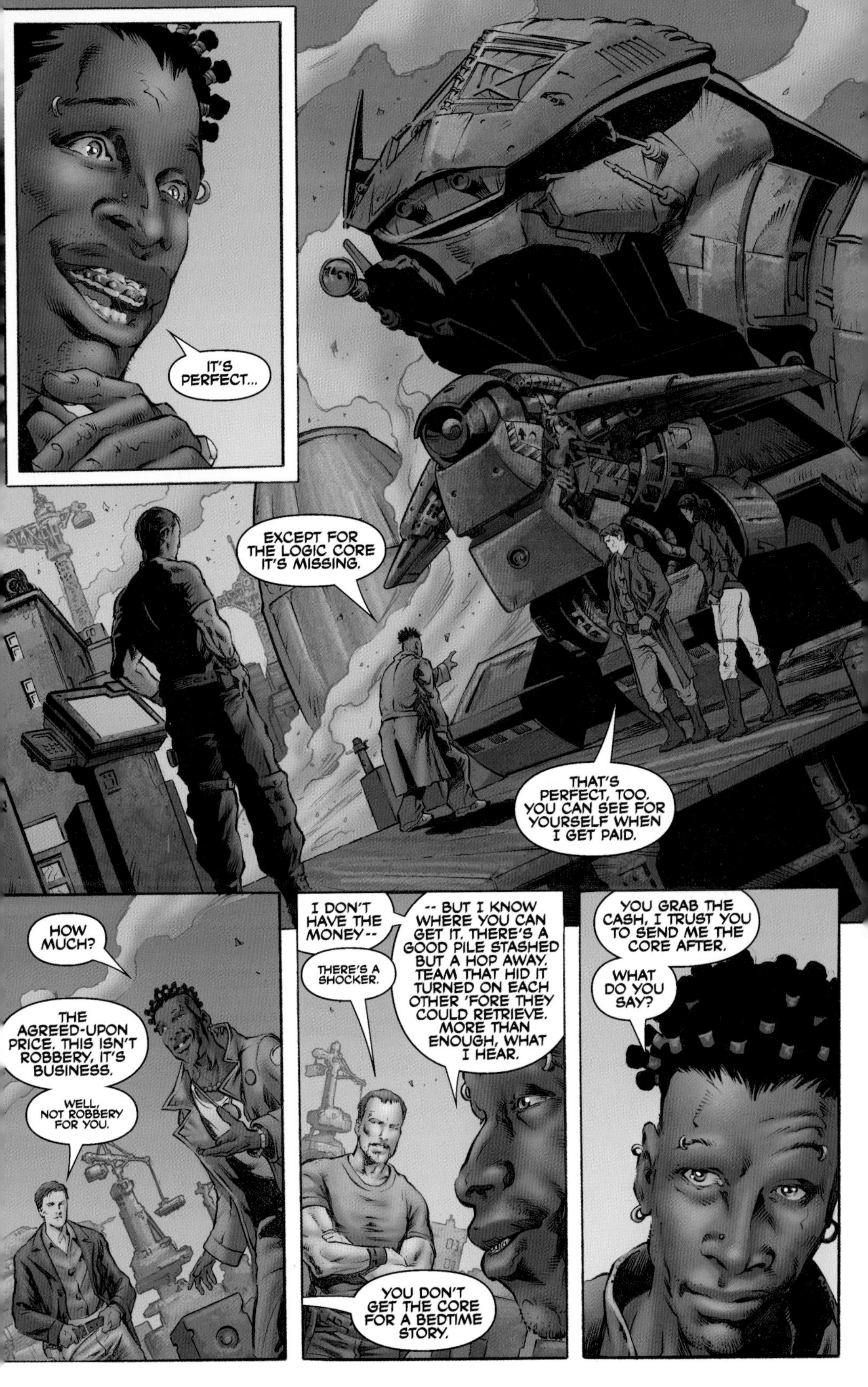
IT'S PERFECT...
EXCEPT FOR THE LOGIC CORE IT'S MISSING.
THAT'S PERFECT, TOO. YOU CAN SEE FOR YOURSELF WHEN I GET PAID.
HOW MUCH?
THE AGREED-UPON PRICE. THIS ISN'T ROBBERY, IT'S BUSINESS.
WELL, NOT ROBBERY FOR YOU.
I DON'T HAVE THE MONEY--
THERE'S A SHOCKER.
-- BUT I KNOW WHERE YOU CAN GET IT. THERE'S A GOOD PILE STASHED BUT A HOP AWAY. TEAM THAT HID IT TURNED ON EACH OTHER 'FORE THEY COULD RETRIEVE. MORE THAN ENOUGH, WHAT I HEAR.
YOU DON'T GET THE CORE FOR A BEDTIME STORY.
YOU GRAB THE CASH, I TRUST YOU TO SEND ME THE CORE AFTER.
WHAT DO YOU SAY?

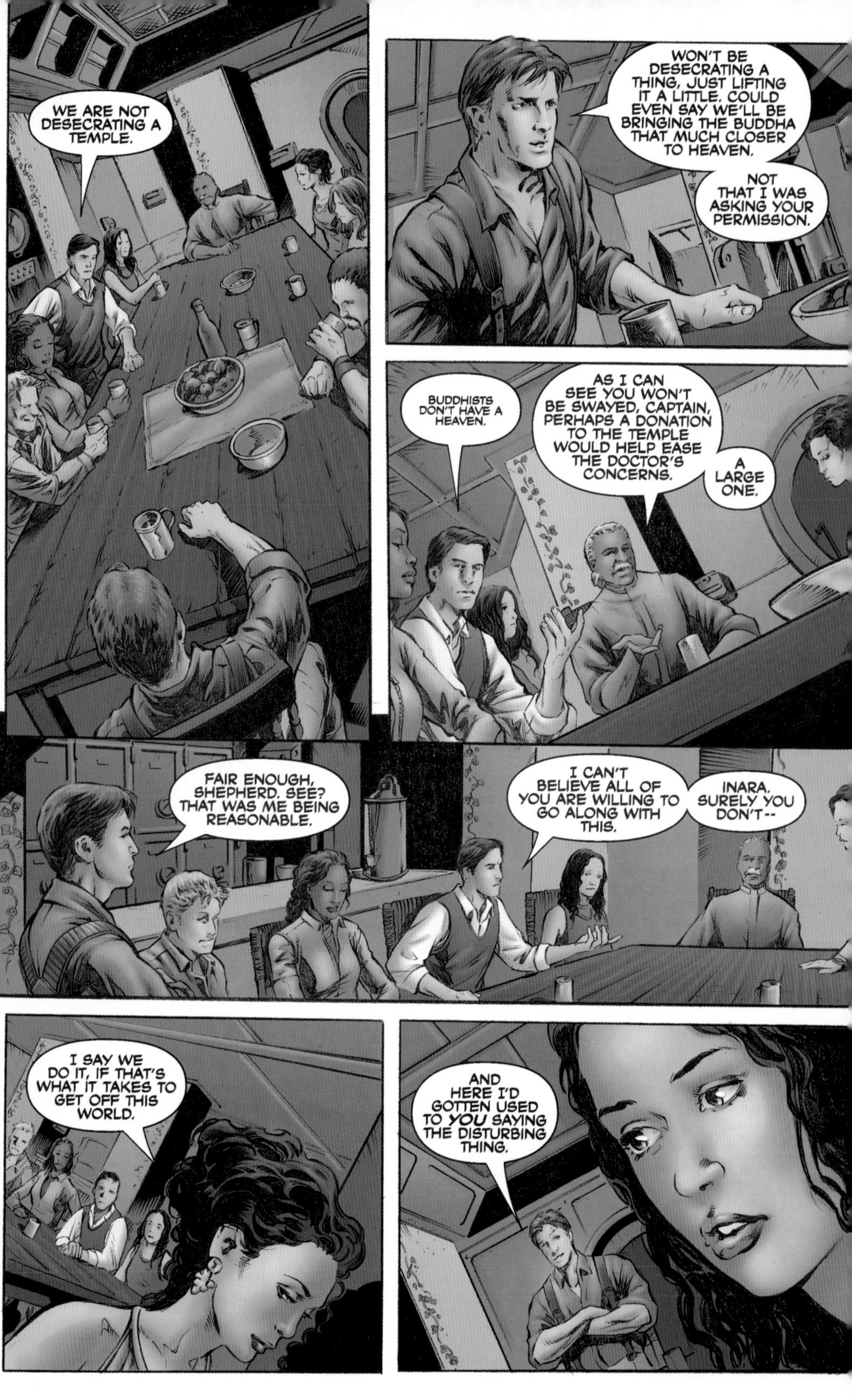
WE ARE NOT DESECRATING A TEMPLE.
WON'T BE DESECRATING A THING, JUST LIFTING IT A LITTLE. COULD EVEN SAY WE'LL BE BRINGING THE BUDDHA THAT MUCH CLOSER TO HEAVEN.
NOT THAT I WAS ASKING YOUR PERMISSION.
BUDDHISTS DON'T HAVE A HEAVEN.
AS I CAN SEE YOU WON'T BE SWAYED, CAPTAIN, PERHAPS A DONATION TO THE TEMPLE WOULD HELP EASE THE DOCTOR'S CONCERNS.
A LARGE ONE.
FAIR ENOUGH, SHEPHERD. SEE? THAT WAS ME BEING REASONABLE.
I CAN'T BELIEVE ALL OF YOU ARE WILLING TO GO ALONG WITH THIS.
INARA, SURELY YOU DON'T--
I SAY WE DO IT, IF THAT'S WHAT IT TAKES TO GET OFF THIS WORLD.
AND HERE I'D GOTTEN USED TO YOU SAYING THE DISTURBING THING.

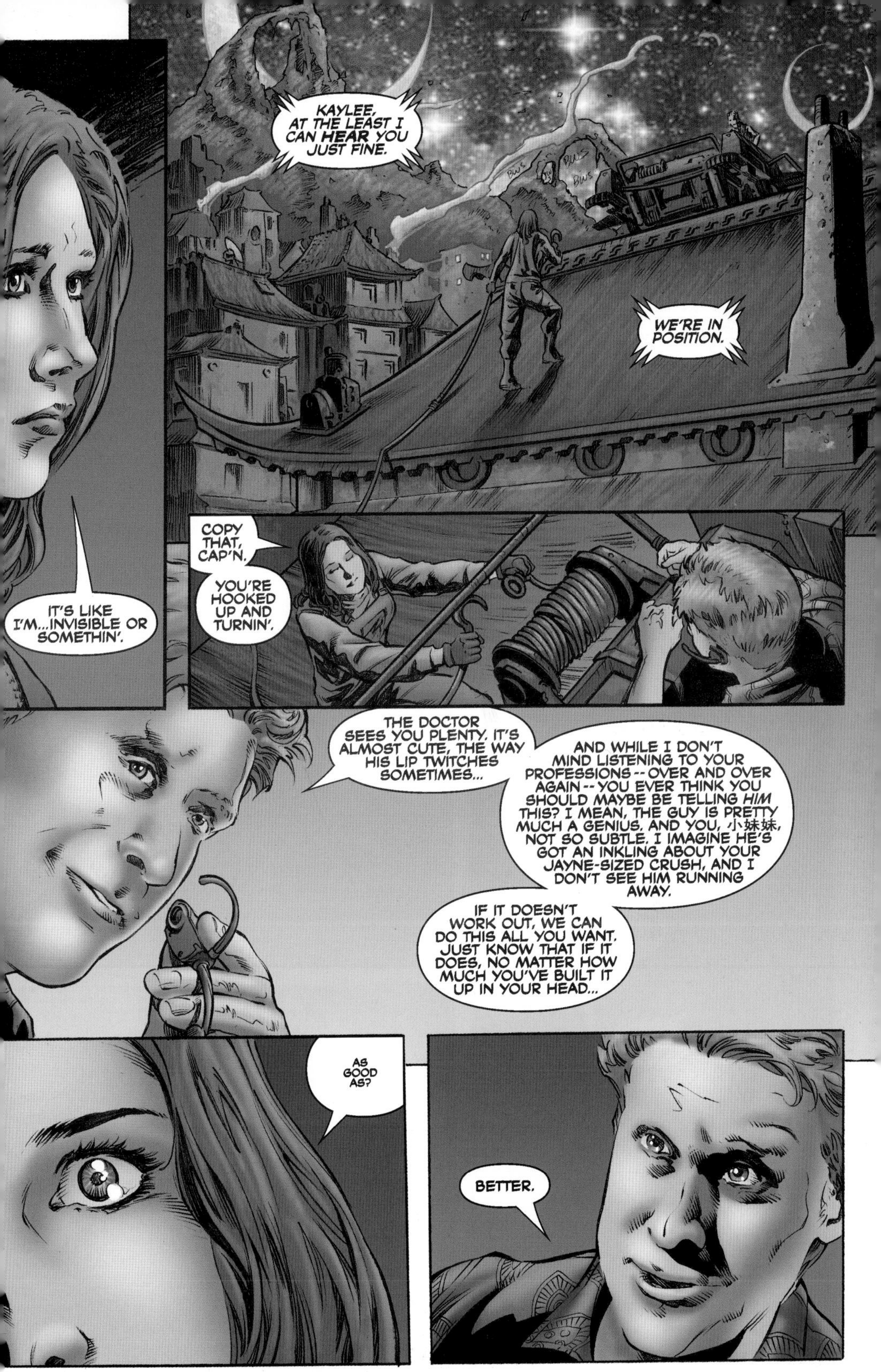
KAYLEE, AT THE LEAST I CAN **HEAR** YOU JUST FINE.
WE'RE IN POSITION.
IT'S LIKE I'M...INVISIBLE OR SOMETHIN'.
COPY THAT, CAP'N.
YOU'RE HOOKED UP AND TURNIN'.
THE DOCTOR SEES YOU PLENTY. IT'S ALMOST CUTE, THE WAY HIS LIP TWITCHES SOMETIMES...
AND WHILE I DON'T MIND LISTENING TO YOUR PROFESSIONS -- OVER AND OVER AGAIN -- YOU EVER THINK YOU SHOULD MAYBE BE TELLING *HIM* THIS? I MEAN, THE GUY IS PRETTY MUCH A GENIUS. AND YOU, 小妹妹, NOT SO SUBTLE. I IMAGINE HE'S GOT AN INKLING ABOUT YOUR JAYNE-SIZED CRUSH, AND I DON'T SEE HIM RUNNING AWAY.
IF IT DOESN'T WORK OUT, WE CAN DO THIS ALL YOU WANT. JUST KNOW THAT IF IT DOES, NO MATTER HOW MUCH YOU'VE BUILT IT UP IN YOUR HEAD...
AS GOOD AS?
BETTER.

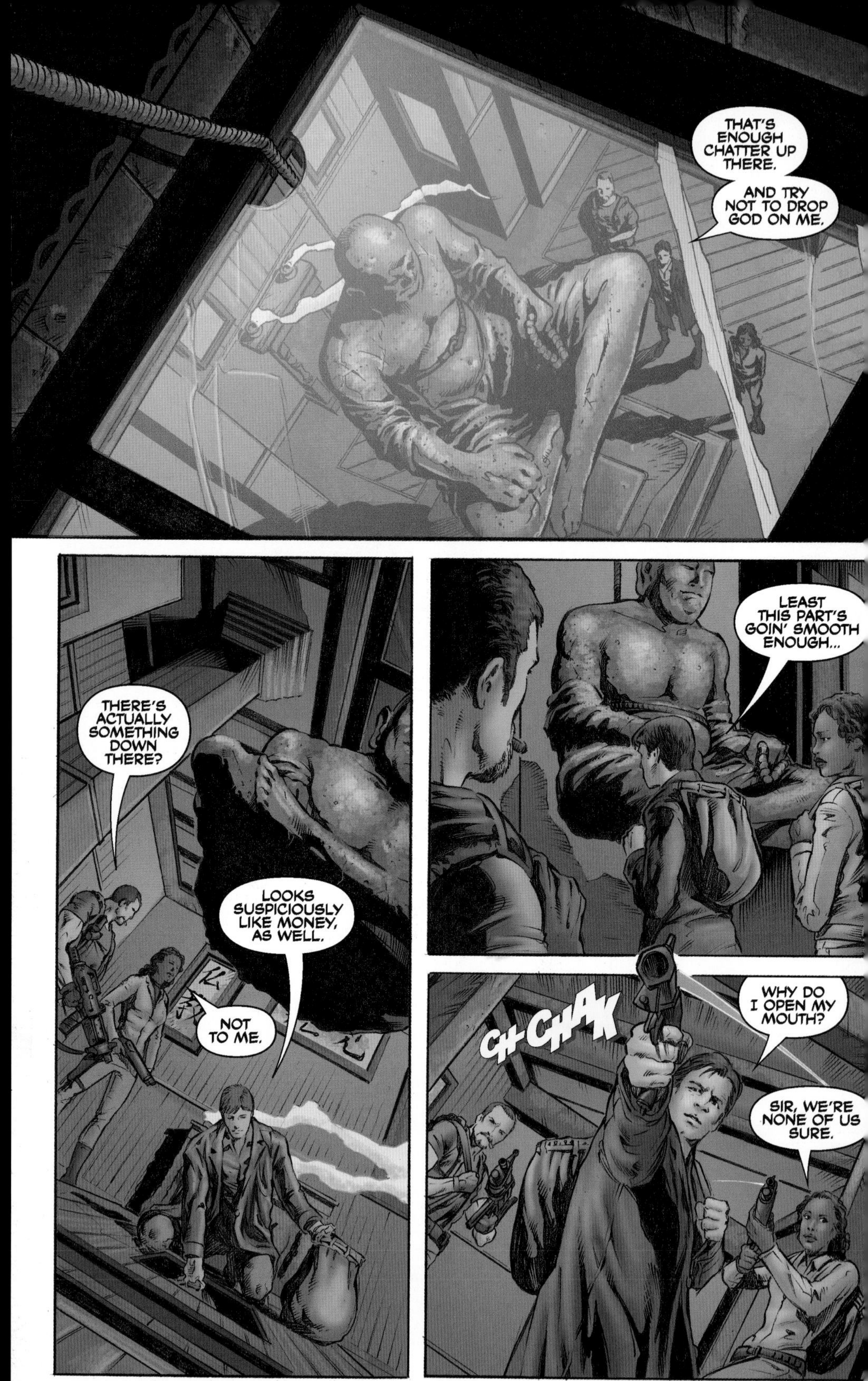
THAT'S ENOUGH CHATTER UP THERE.
AND TRY NOT TO DROP GOD ON ME.
THERE'S ACTUALLY SOMETHING DOWN THERE?
LOOKS SUSPICIOUSLY LIKE MONEY, AS WELL.
NOT TO ME.
LEAST THIS PART'S GOIN' SMOOTH ENOUGH...
CH-CHAK
WHY DO I OPEN MY MOUTH?
SIR, WE'RE NONE OF US SURE.

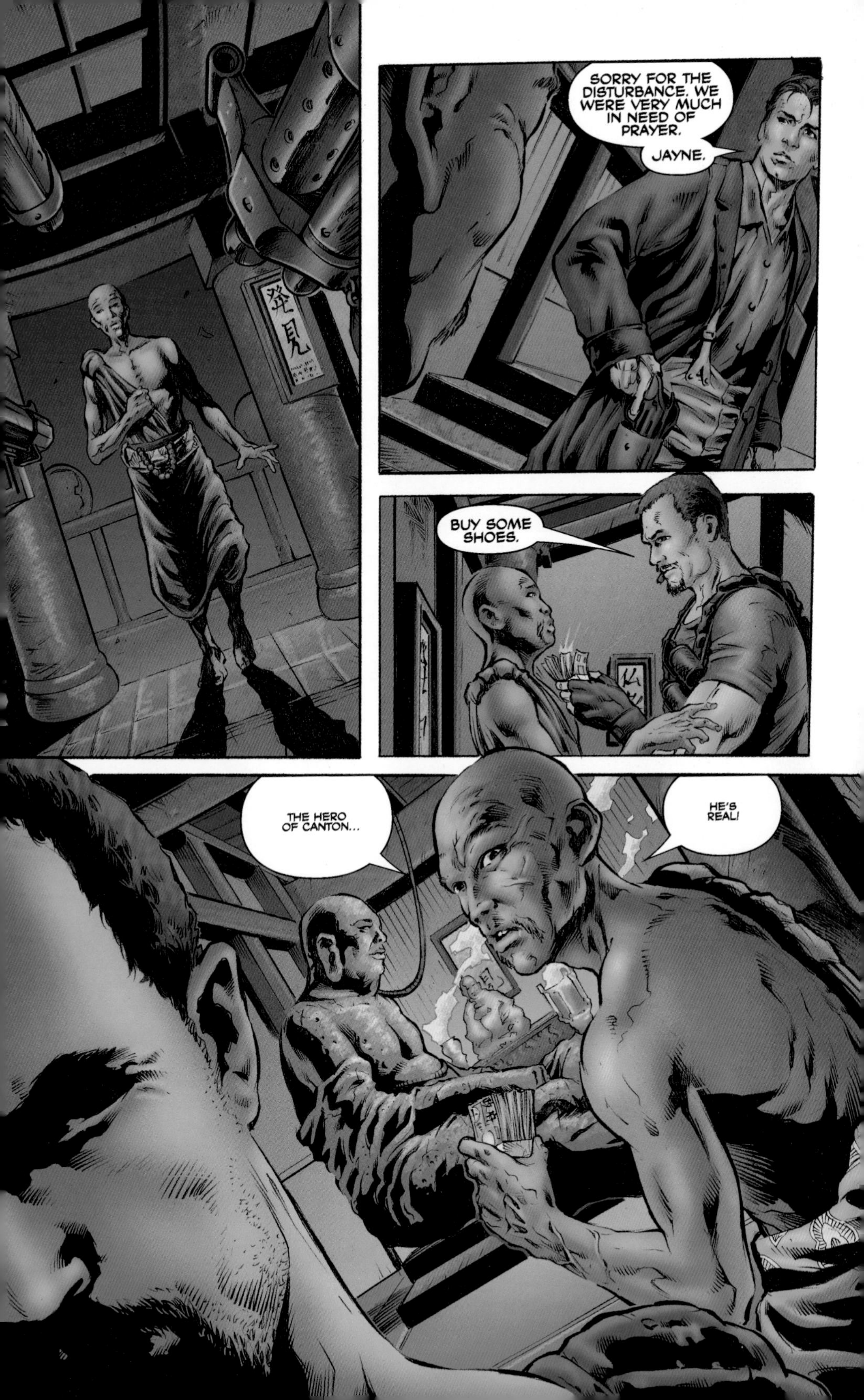
SORRY FOR THE DISTURBANCE. WE WERE VERY MUCH IN NEED OF PRAYER.
JAYNE.
BUY SOME SHOES.
THE HERO OF CANTON...
HE'S REAL!

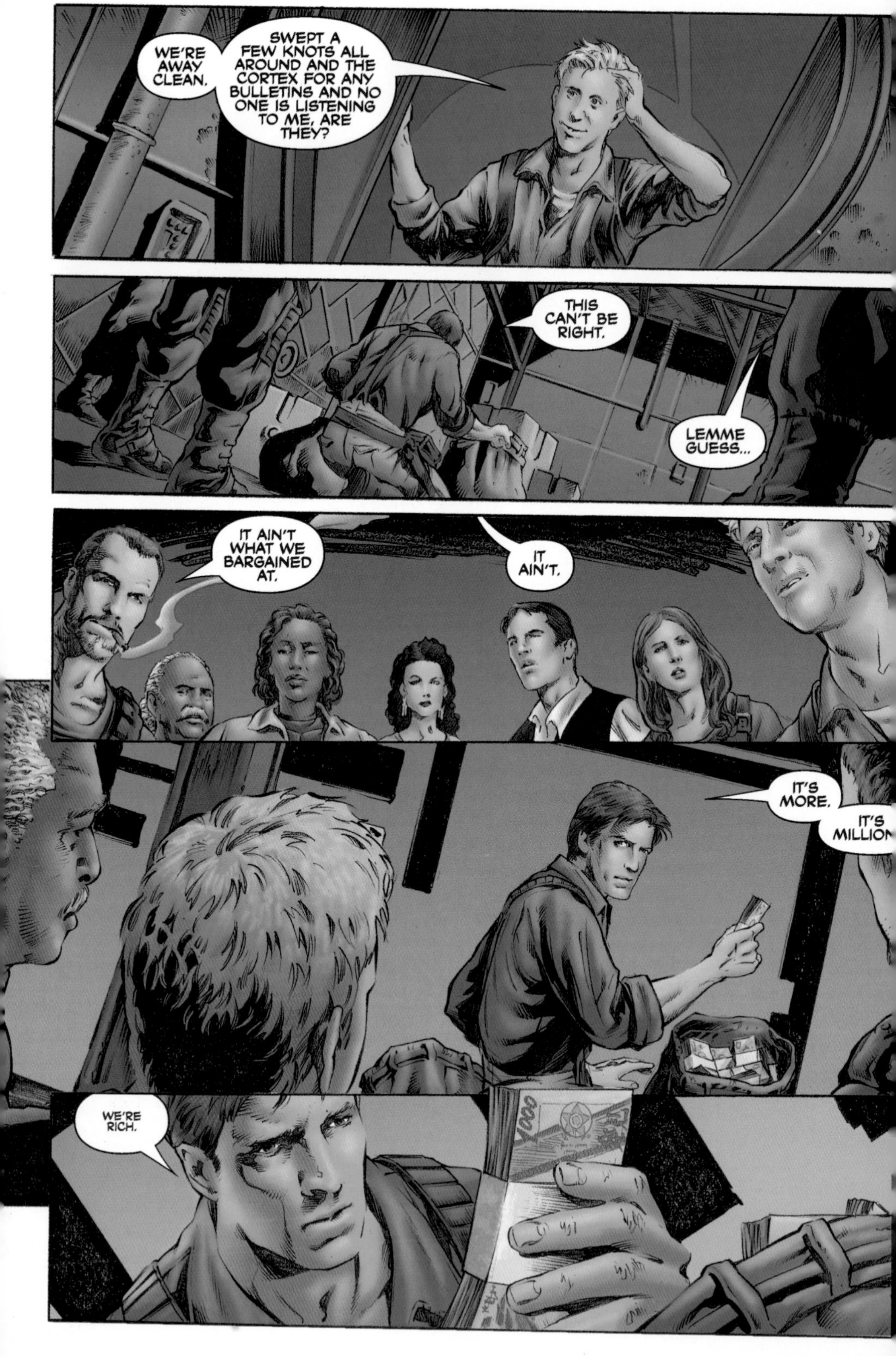
WE'RE AWAY CLEAN.
SWEPT A FEW KNOTS ALL AROUND AND THE CORTEX FOR ANY BULLETINS AND NO ONE IS LISTENING TO ME, ARE THEY?
THIS CAN'T BE RIGHT.
LEMME GUESS...
IT AIN'T WHAT WE BARGAINED AT.
IT AIN'T.
IT'S MORE.
IT'S MILLION
WE'RE RICH.

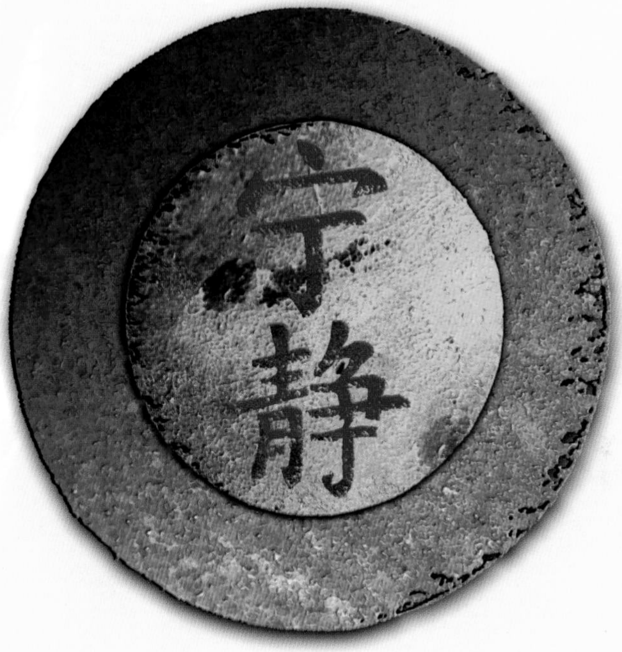
守静

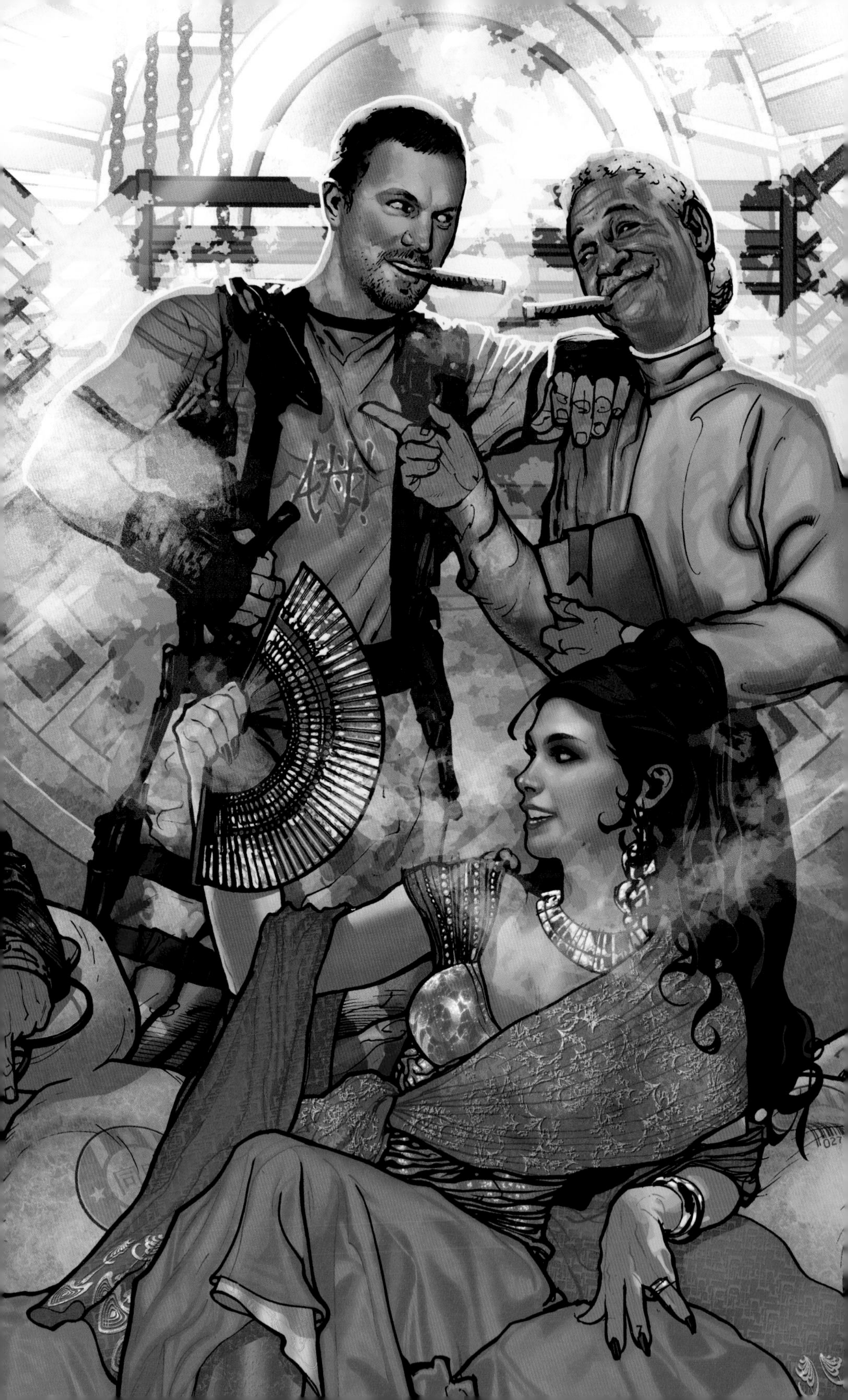

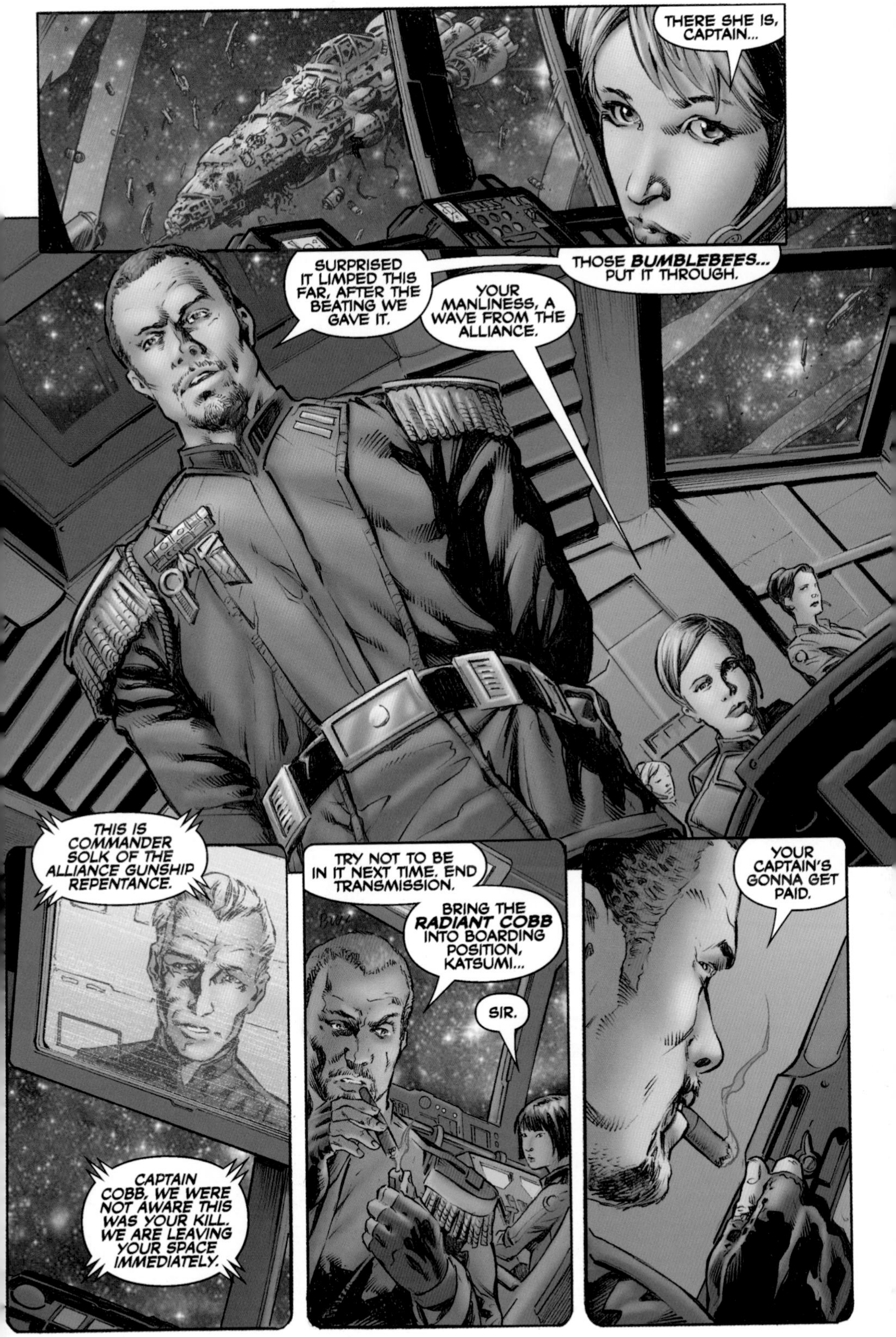
THERE SHE IS, CAPTAIN...
SURPRISED IT LIMPED THIS FAR, AFTER THE BEATING WE GAVE IT.
THOSE BUMBLEBEES... PUT IT THROUGH.
YOUR MANLINESS, A WAVE FROM THE ALLIANCE.
THIS IS COMMANDER SOLK OF THE ALLIANCE GUNSHIP REPENTANCE.
CAPTAIN COBB, WE WERE NOT AWARE THIS WAS YOUR KILL. WE ARE LEAVING YOUR SPACE IMMEDIATELY.
TRY NOT TO BE IN IT NEXT TIME. END TRANSMISSION.
BRING THE RADIANT COBB INTO BOARDING POSITION, KATSUMI...
SIR.
YOUR CAPTAIN'S GONNA GET PAID.

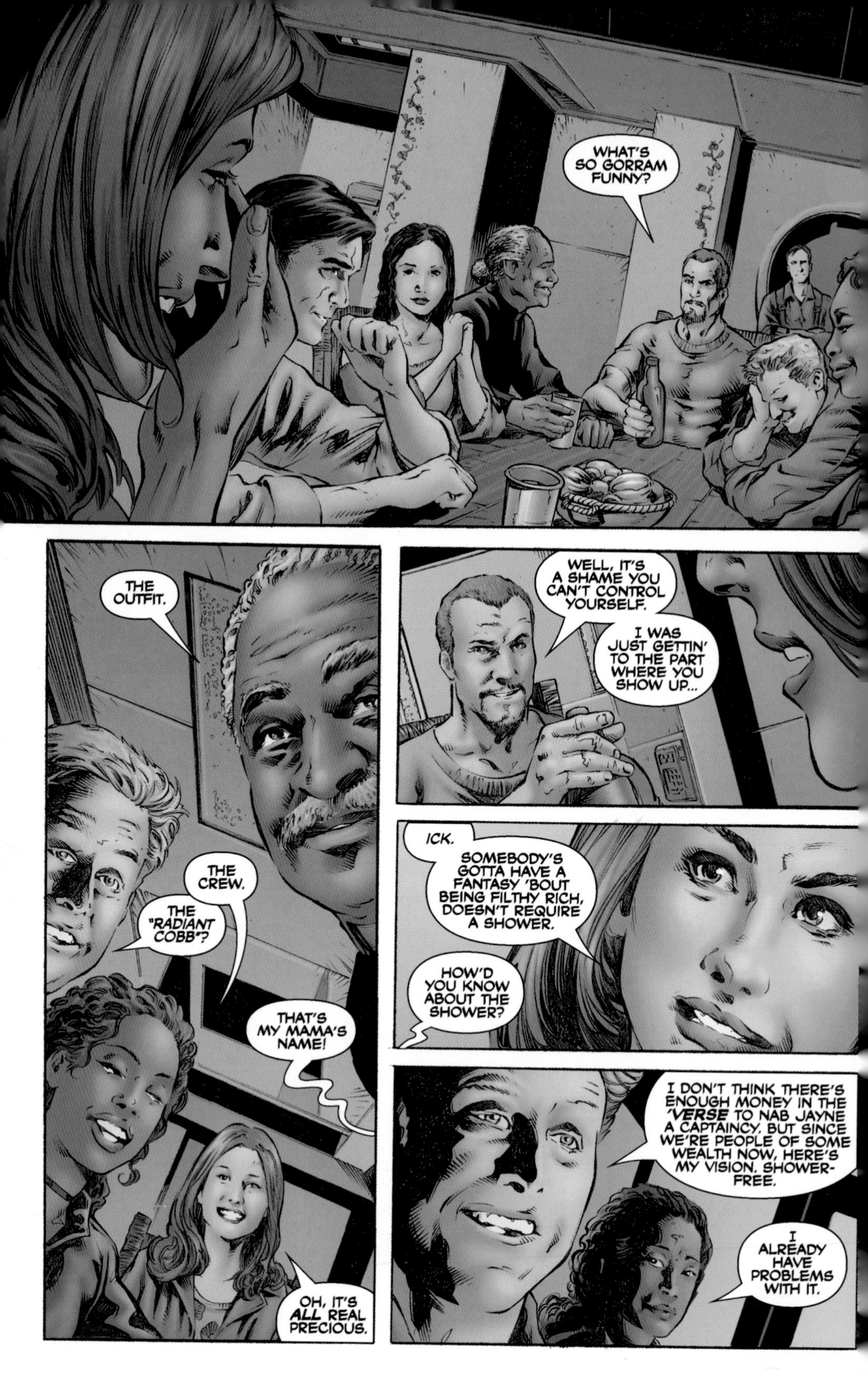
WHAT'S SO GORRAM FUNNY?
THE OUTFIT.
THE CREW.
THE "RADIANT COBB"?
THAT'S MY MAMA'S NAME!
OH, IT'S ALL REAL PRECIOUS.
WELL, IT'S A SHAME YOU CAN'T CONTROL YOURSELF.
I WAS JUST GETTIN' TO THE PART WHERE YOU SHOW UP...
ICK.
SOMEBODY'S GOTTA HAVE A FANTASY 'BOUT BEING FILTHY RICH, DOESN'T REQUIRE A SHOWER.
HOW'D YOU KNOW ABOUT THE SHOWER?
I DON'T THINK THERE'S ENOUGH MONEY IN THE 'VERSE TO NAB JAYNE A CAPTAINCY. BUT SINCE WE'RE PEOPLE OF SOME WEALTH NOW, HERE'S MY VISION. SHOWER-FREE.
I ALREADY HAVE PROBLEMS WITH IT.

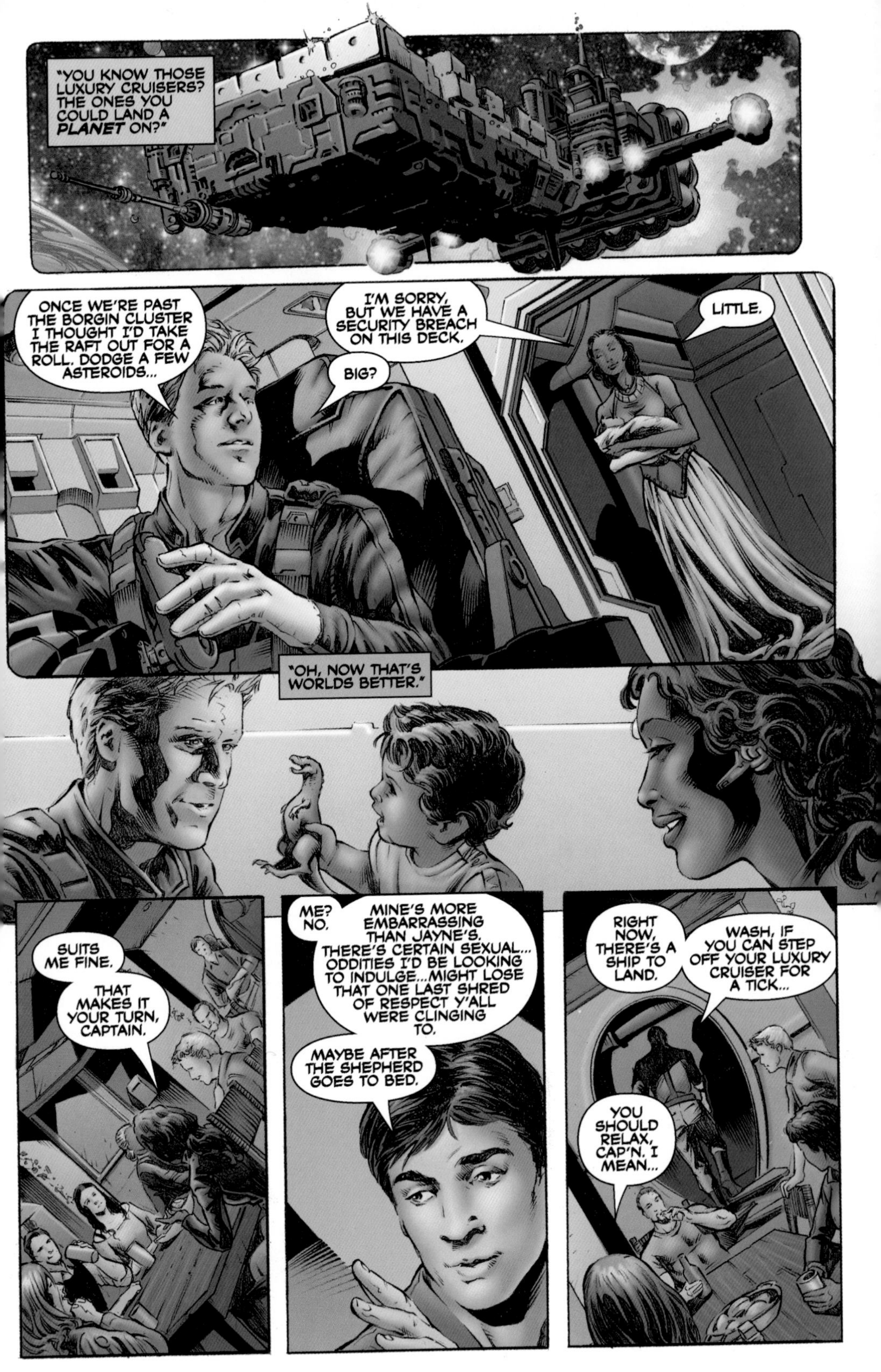
"YOU KNOW THOSE LUXURY CRUISERS? THE ONES YOU COULD LAND A *PLANET* ON?"
ONCE WE'RE PAST THE BORGIN CLUSTER I THOUGHT I'D TAKE THE RAFT OUT FOR A ROLL. DODGE A FEW ASTEROIDS...
I'M SORRY, BUT WE HAVE A SECURITY BREACH ON THIS DECK.
BIG?
LITTLE.
"OH, NOW THAT'S WORLDS BETTER."
SUITS ME FINE.
THAT MAKES IT YOUR TURN, CAPTAIN.
ME? NO.
MINE'S MORE EMBARRASSING THAN JAYNE'S. THERE'S CERTAIN SEXUAL... ODDITIES I'D BE LOOKING TO INDULGE...MIGHT LOSE THAT ONE LAST SHRED OF RESPECT Y'ALL WERE CLINGING TO.
MAYBE AFTER THE SHEPHERD GOES TO BED.
RIGHT NOW, THERE'S A SHIP TO LAND.
WASH, IF YOU CAN STEP OFF YOUR LUXURY CRUISER FOR A TICK...
YOU SHOULD RELAX, CAP'N. I MEAN...

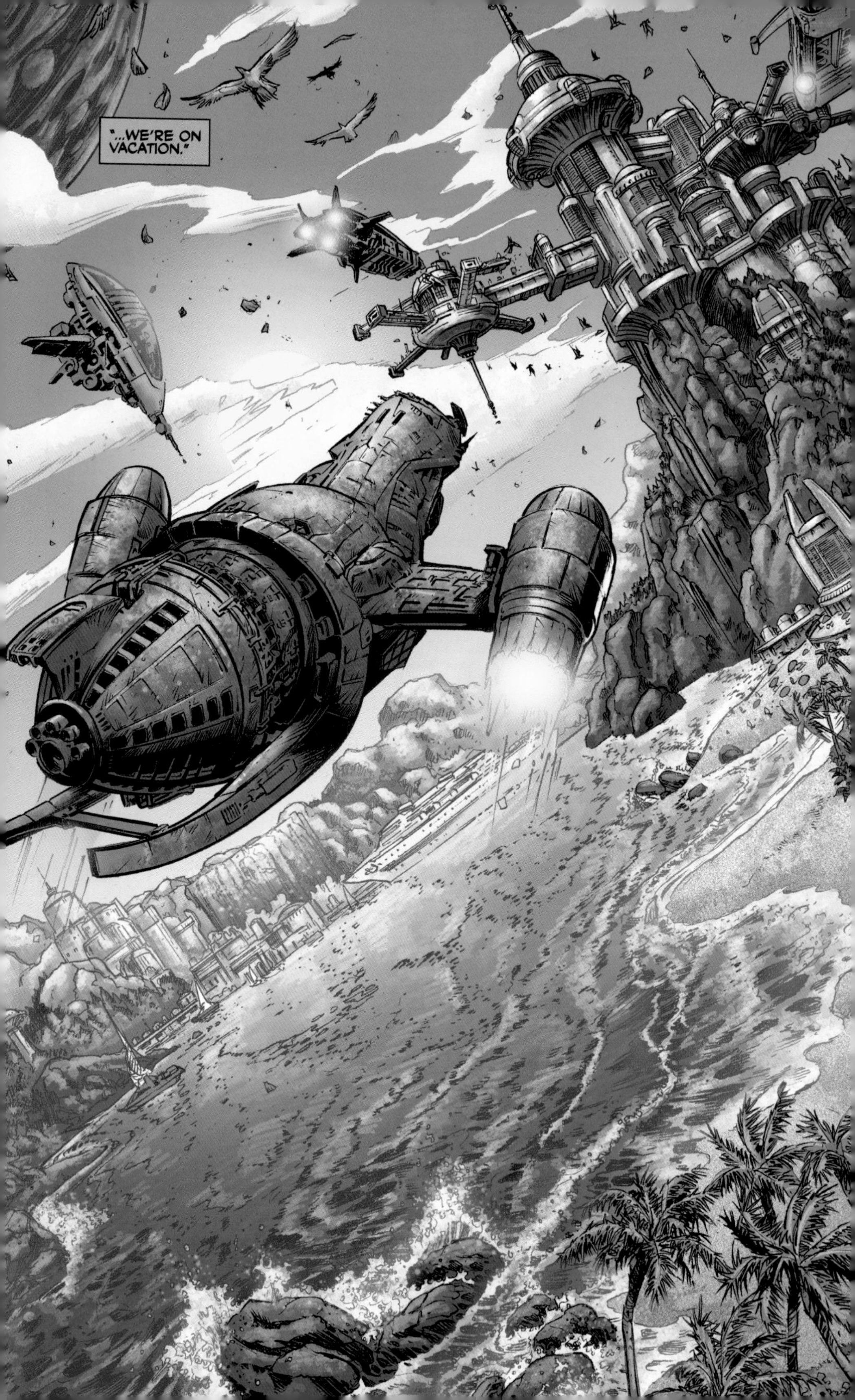
"...WE'RE ON VACATION."

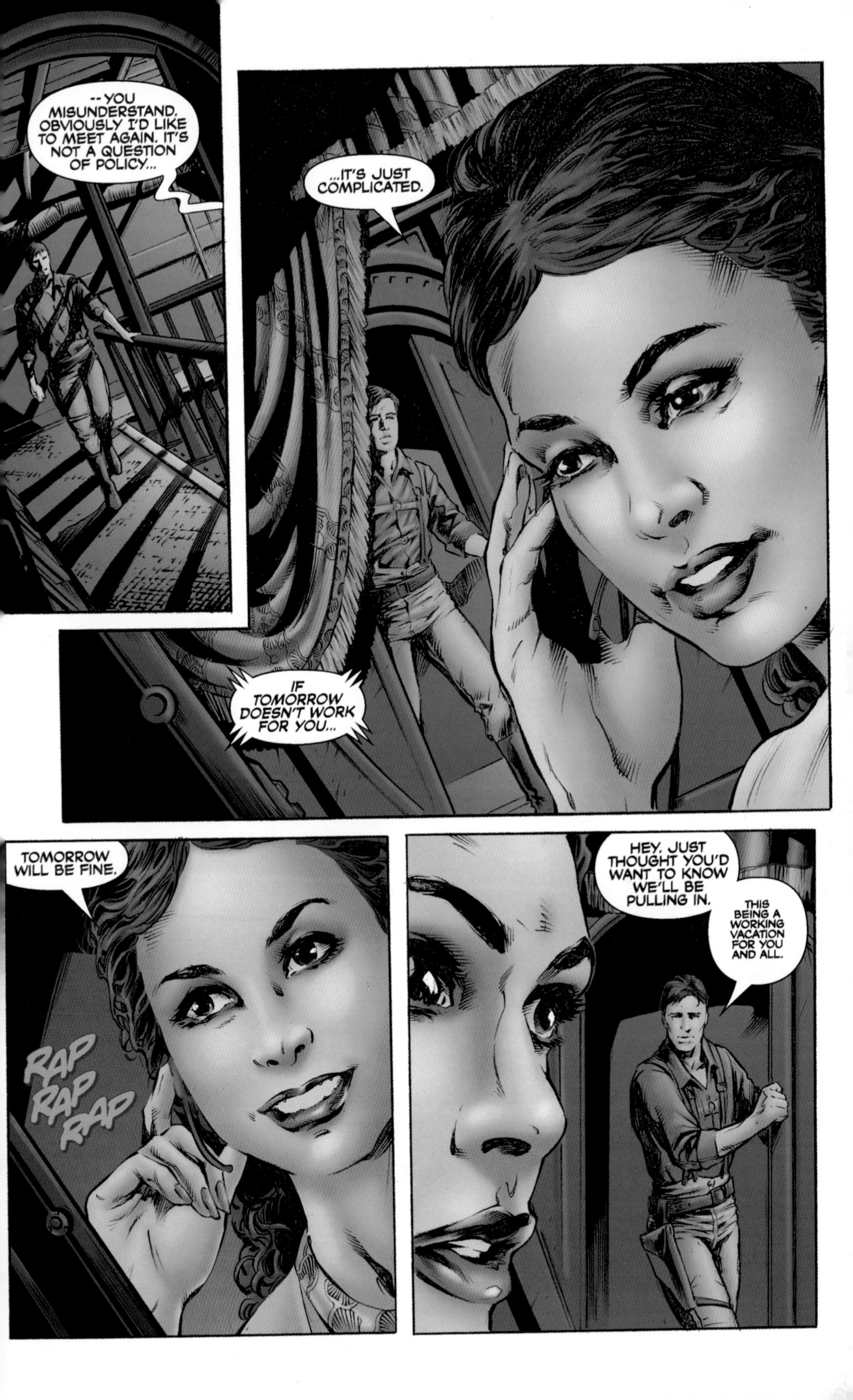
--YOU MISUNDERSTAND. OBVIOUSLY I'D LIKE TO MEET AGAIN. IT'S NOT A QUESTION OF POLICY...
...IT'S JUST COMPLICATED.
IF TOMORROW DOESN'T WORK FOR YOU...
TOMORROW WILL BE FINE.
RAP RAP RAP
HEY, JUST THOUGHT YOU'D WANT TO KNOW WE'LL BE PULLING IN.
THIS BEING A WORKING VACATION FOR YOU AND ALL.

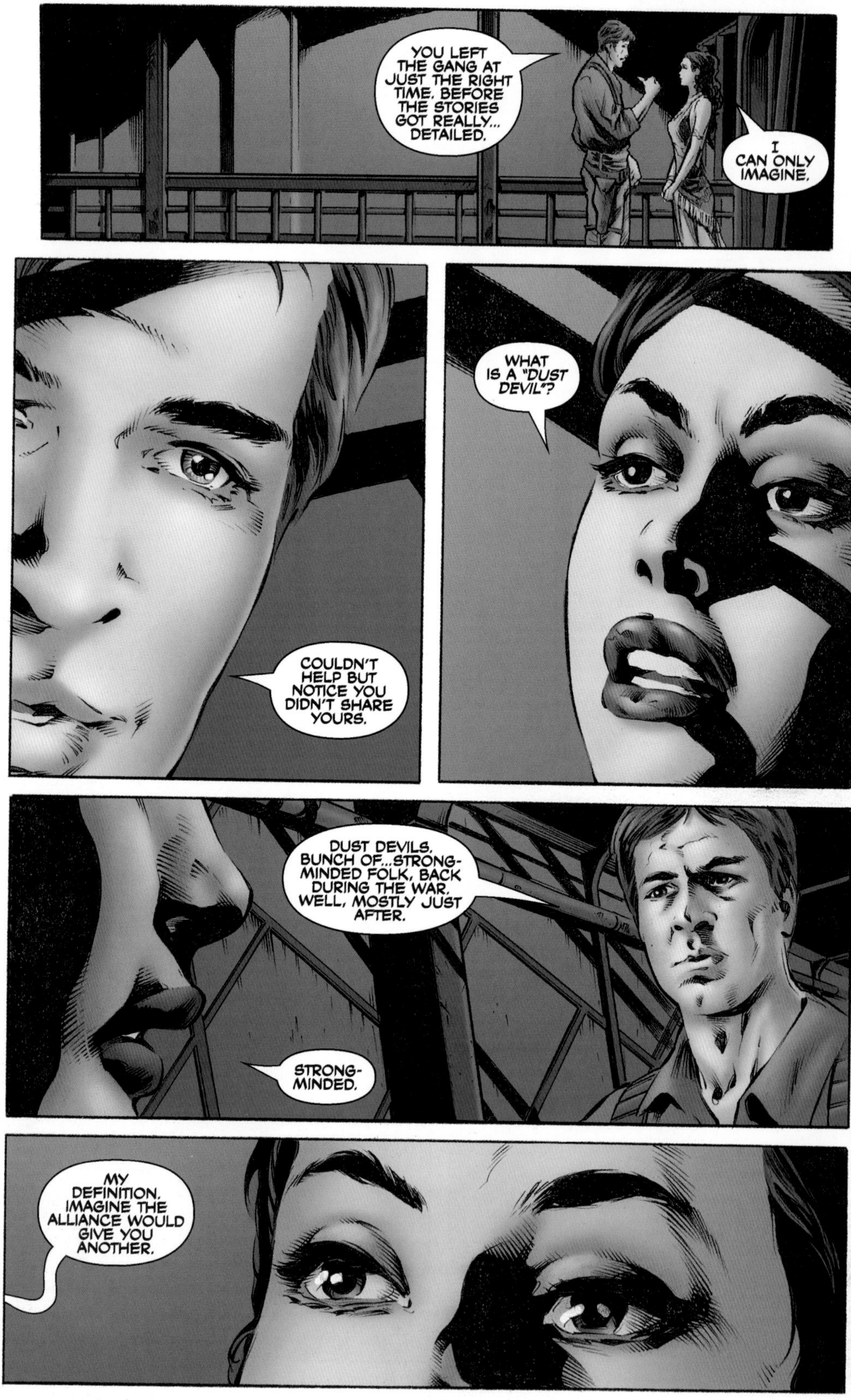
YOU LEFT THE GANG AT JUST THE RIGHT TIME. BEFORE THE STORIES GOT REALLY... DETAILED.
I CAN ONLY IMAGINE.
COULDN'T HELP BUT NOTICE YOU DIDN'T SHARE YOURS.
WHAT IS A "DUST DEVIL"?
DUST DEVILS. BUNCH OF...STRONG-MINDED FOLK, BACK DURING THE WAR. WELL, MOSTLY JUST AFTER.
STRONG-MINDED.
MY DEFINITION. IMAGINE THE ALLIANCE WOULD GIVE YOU ANOTHER.

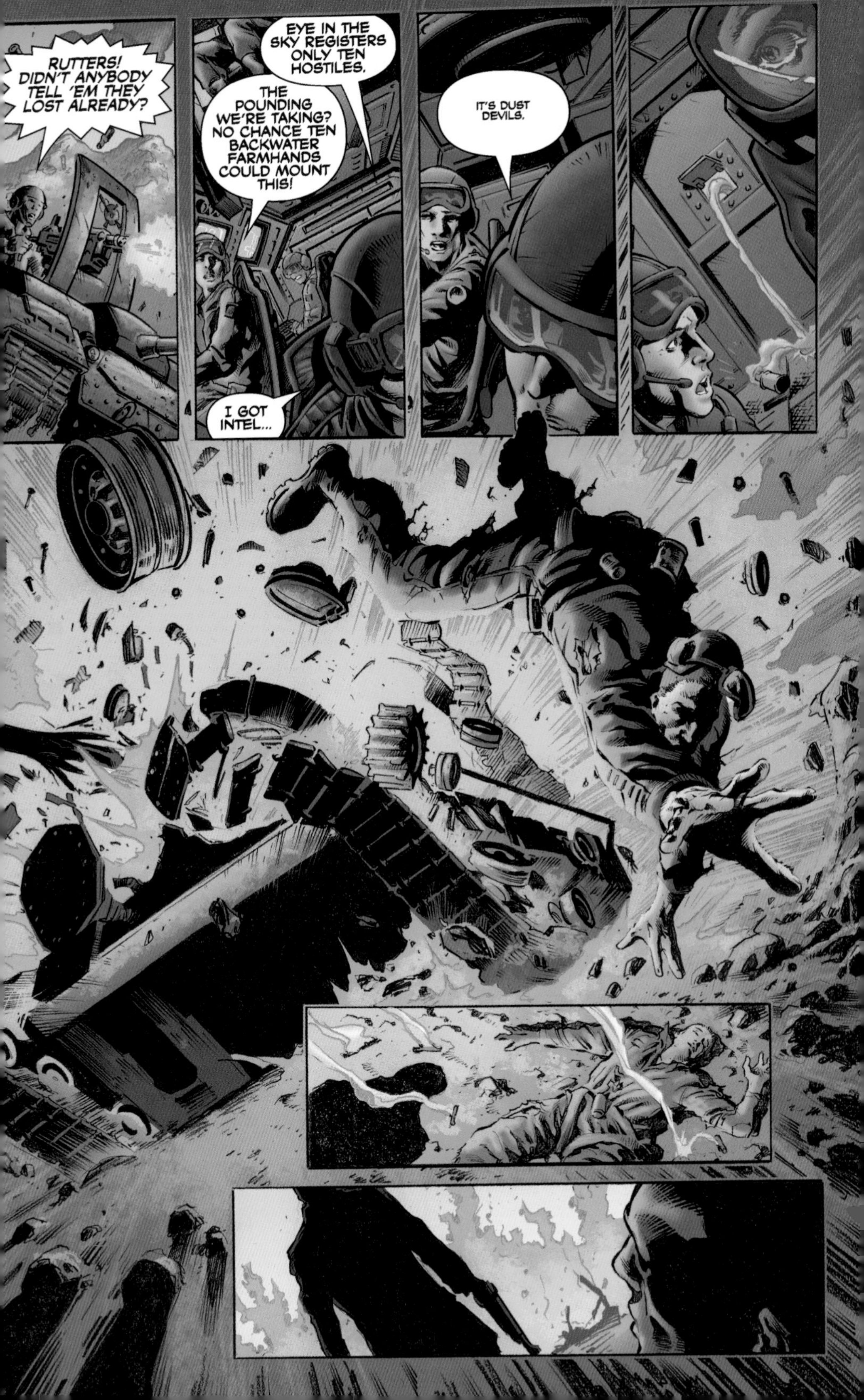
RUTTERS! DIDN'T ANYBODY TELL 'EM THEY LOST ALREADY?
EYE IN THE SKY REGISTERS ONLY TEN HOSTILES.
THE POUNDING WE'RE TAKING? NO CHANCE TEN BACKWATER FARMHANDS COULD MOUNT THIS!
I GOT INTEL...
IT'S DUST DEVILS.

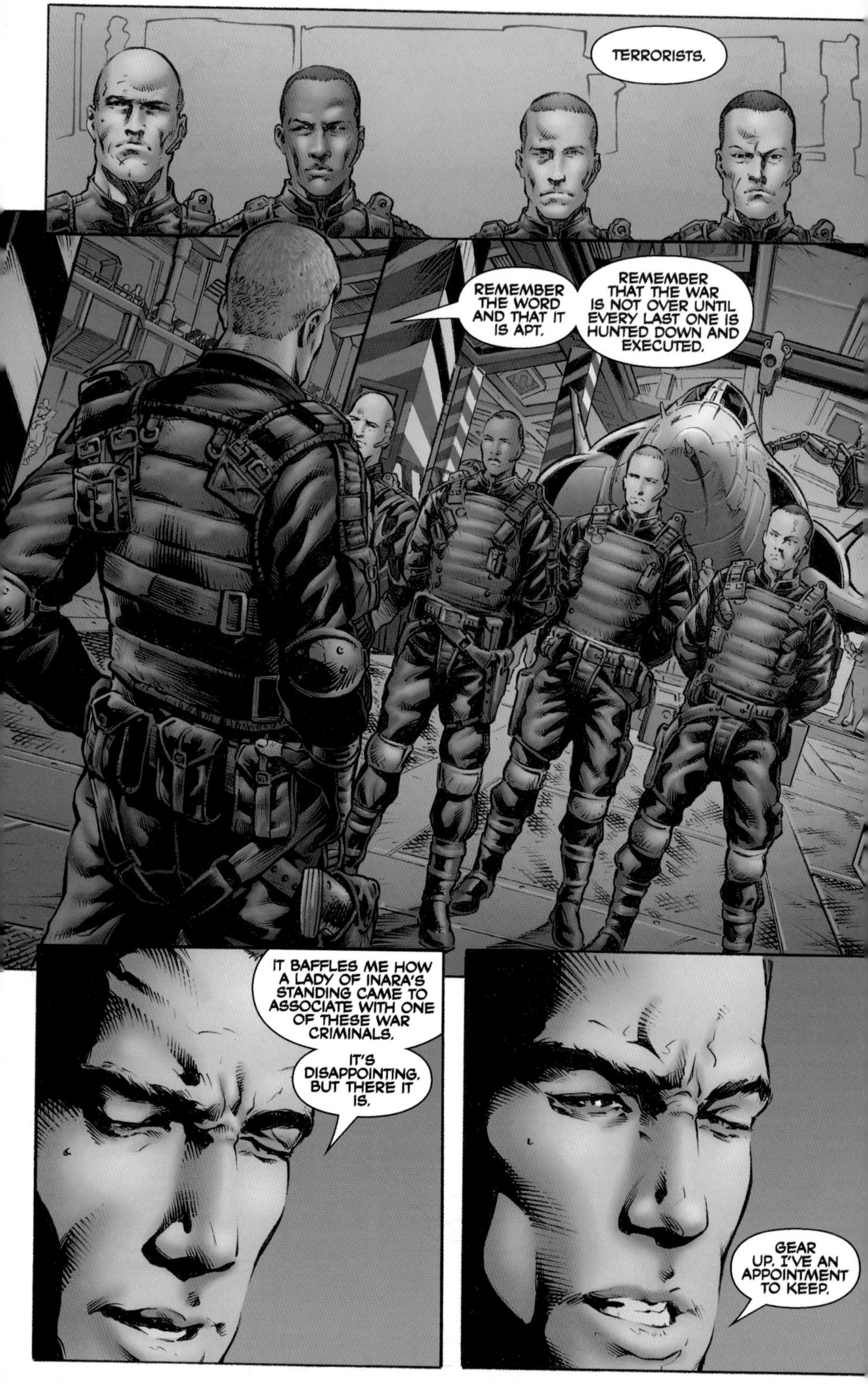
TERRORISTS.
REMEMBER THE WORD AND THAT IT IS APT.
REMEMBER THAT THE WAR IS NOT OVER UNTIL EVERY LAST ONE IS HUNTED DOWN AND EXECUTED.
IT BAFFLES ME HOW A LADY OF INARA'S STANDING CAME TO ASSOCIATE WITH ONE OF THESE WAR CRIMINALS.
IT'S DISAPPOINTING. BUT THERE IT IS.
GEAR UP. I'VE AN APPOINTMENT TO KEEP.

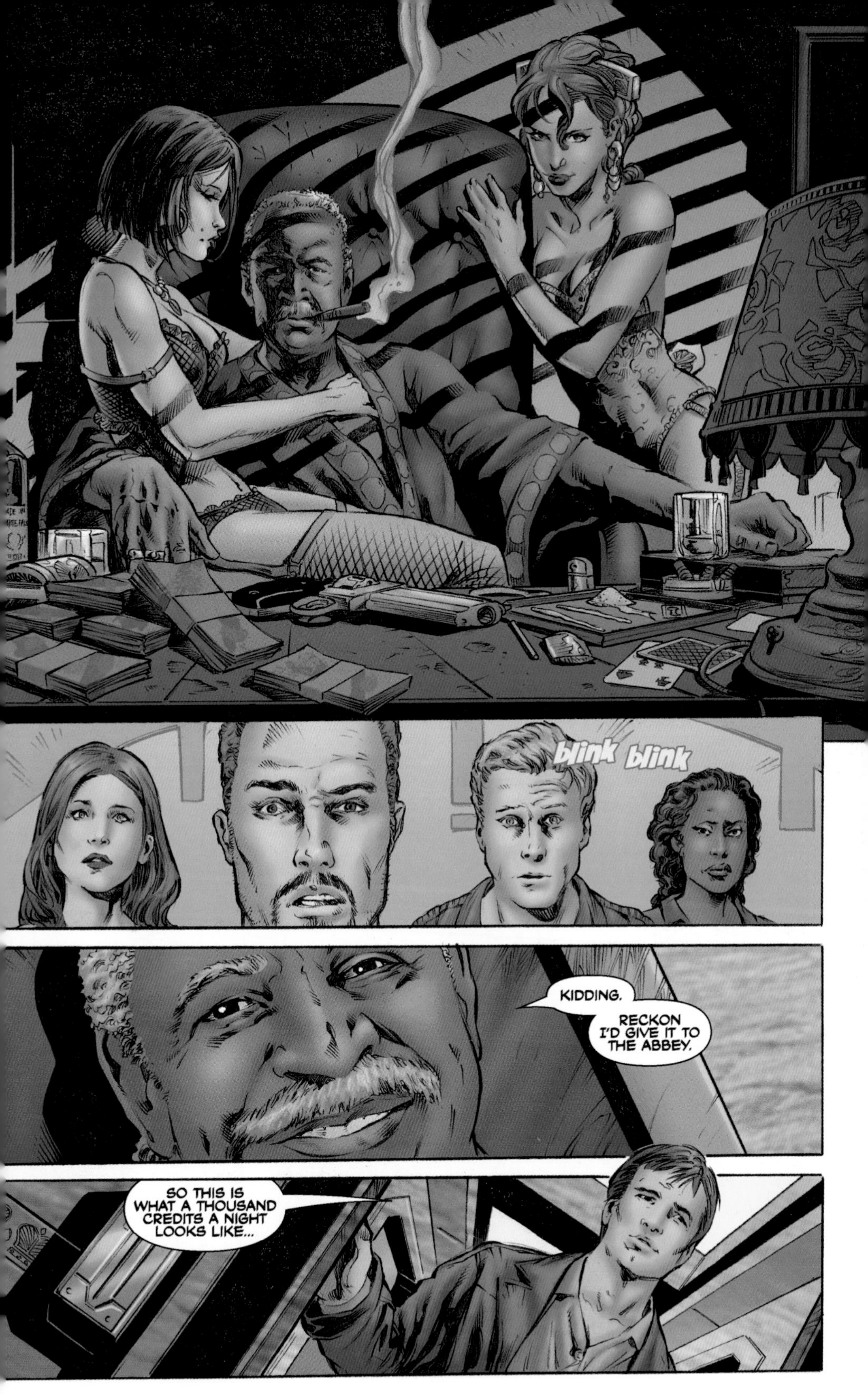
blink blink
KIDDING.
RECKON I'D GIVE IT TO THE ABBEY.
SO THIS IS WHAT A THOUSAND CREDITS A NIGHT LOOKS LIKE...

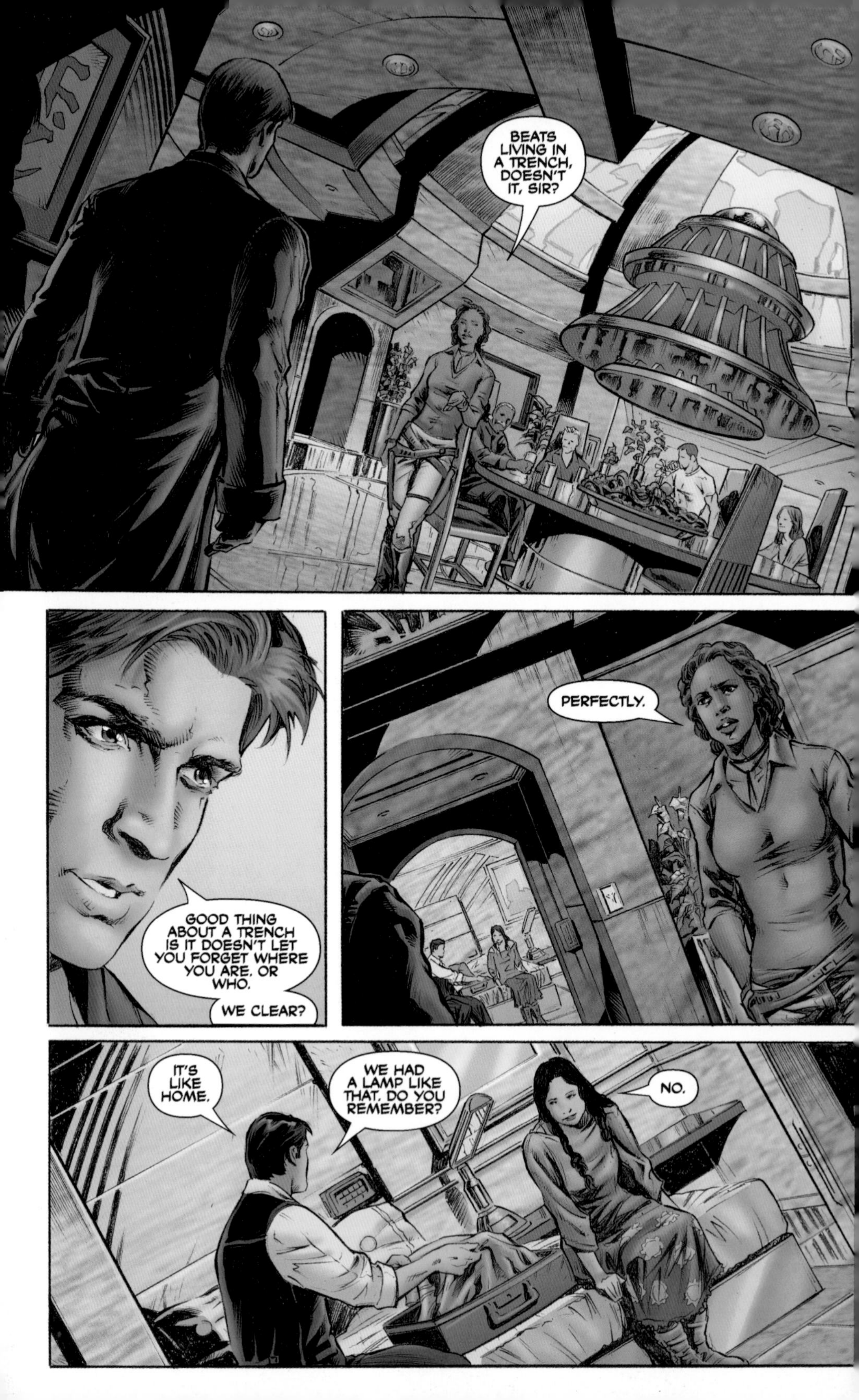
BEATS LIVING IN A TRENCH, DOESN'T IT, SIR?
GOOD THING ABOUT A TRENCH IS IT DOESN'T LET YOU FORGET WHERE YOU ARE. OR WHO.
WE CLEAR?
PERFECTLY.
IT'S LIKE HOME.
WE HAD A LAMP LIKE THAT. DO YOU REMEMBER?
NO.

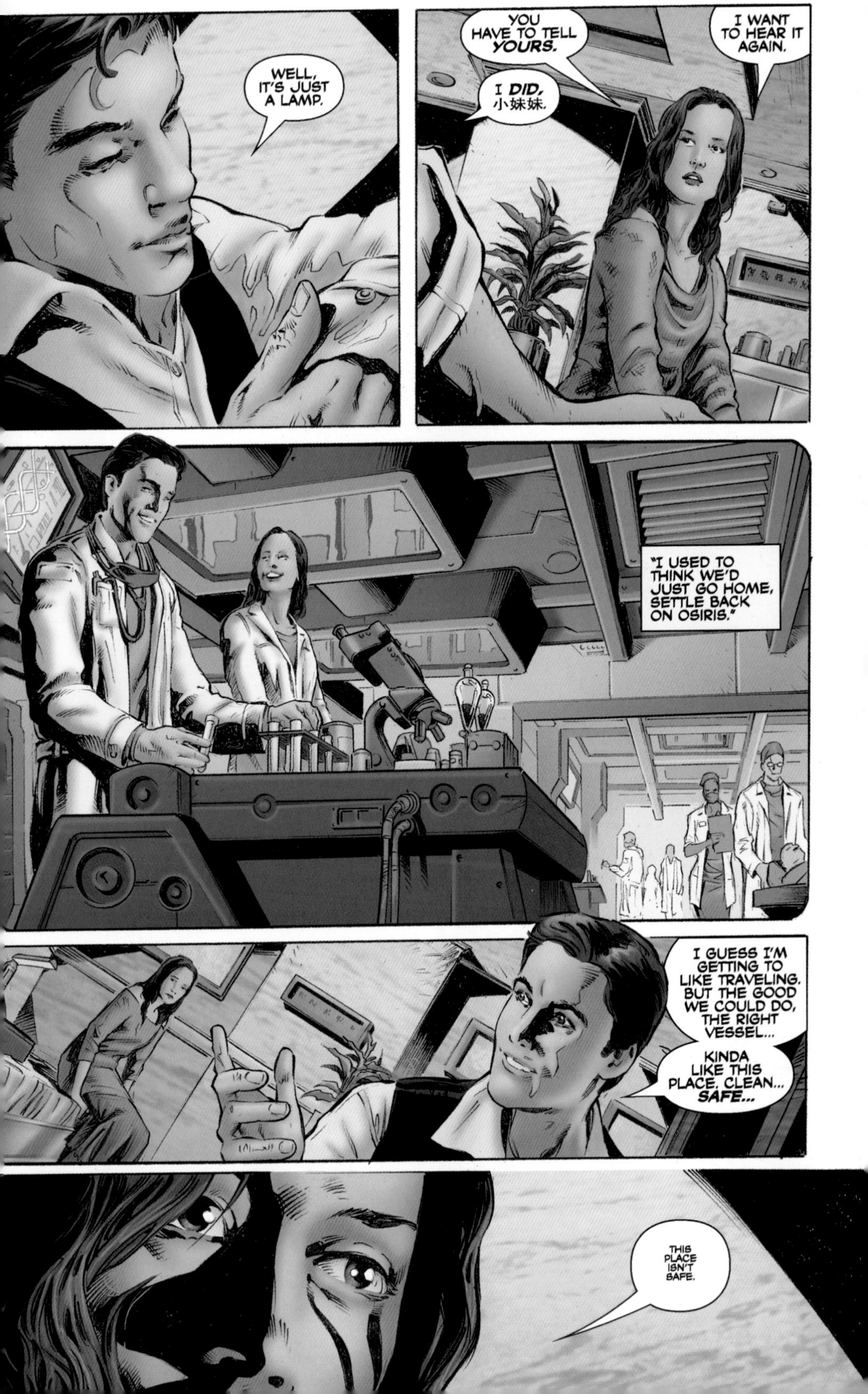

WELL, IT'S JUST A LAMP.
YOU HAVE TO TELL *YOURS.*
I *DID,* 小妹妹.
I WANT TO HEAR IT AGAIN.
"I USED TO THINK WE'D JUST GO HOME, SETTLE BACK ON OSIRIS."
I GUESS I'M GETTING TO LIKE TRAVELING. BUT THE GOOD WE COULD DO, THE RIGHT VESSEL...
KINDA LIKE THIS PLACE, CLEAN... *SAFE...*
THIS PLACE ISN'T SAFE.

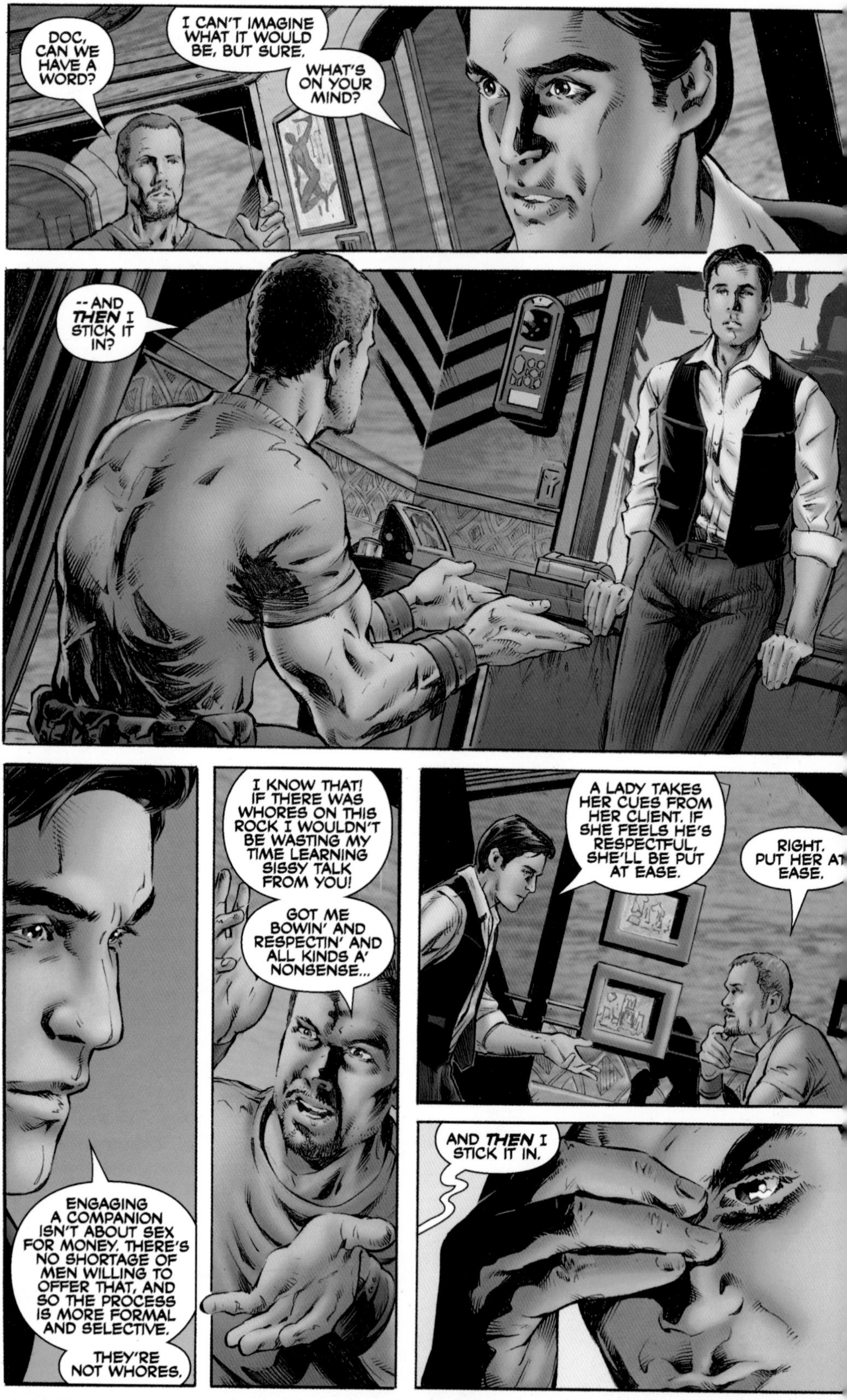
DOC, CAN WE HAVE A WORD?
I CAN'T IMAGINE WHAT IT WOULD BE, BUT SURE.
WHAT'S ON YOUR MIND?
--AND *THEN* I STICK IT IN?
ENGAGING A COMPANION ISN'T ABOUT SEX FOR MONEY. THERE'S NO SHORTAGE OF MEN WILLING TO OFFER THAT, AND SO THE PROCESS IS MORE FORMAL AND SELECTIVE.
THEY'RE NOT WHORES.
I KNOW THAT! IF THERE WAS WHORES ON THIS ROCK I WOULDN'T BE WASTING MY TIME LEARNING SISSY TALK FROM YOU!
GOT ME BOWIN' AND RESPECTIN' AND ALL KINDS A' NONSENSE...
A LADY TAKES HER CUES FROM HER CLIENT. IF SHE FEELS HE'S RESPECTFUL, SHE'LL BE PUT AT EASE.
RIGHT. PUT HER AT EASE.
AND *THEN* I STICK IT IN.

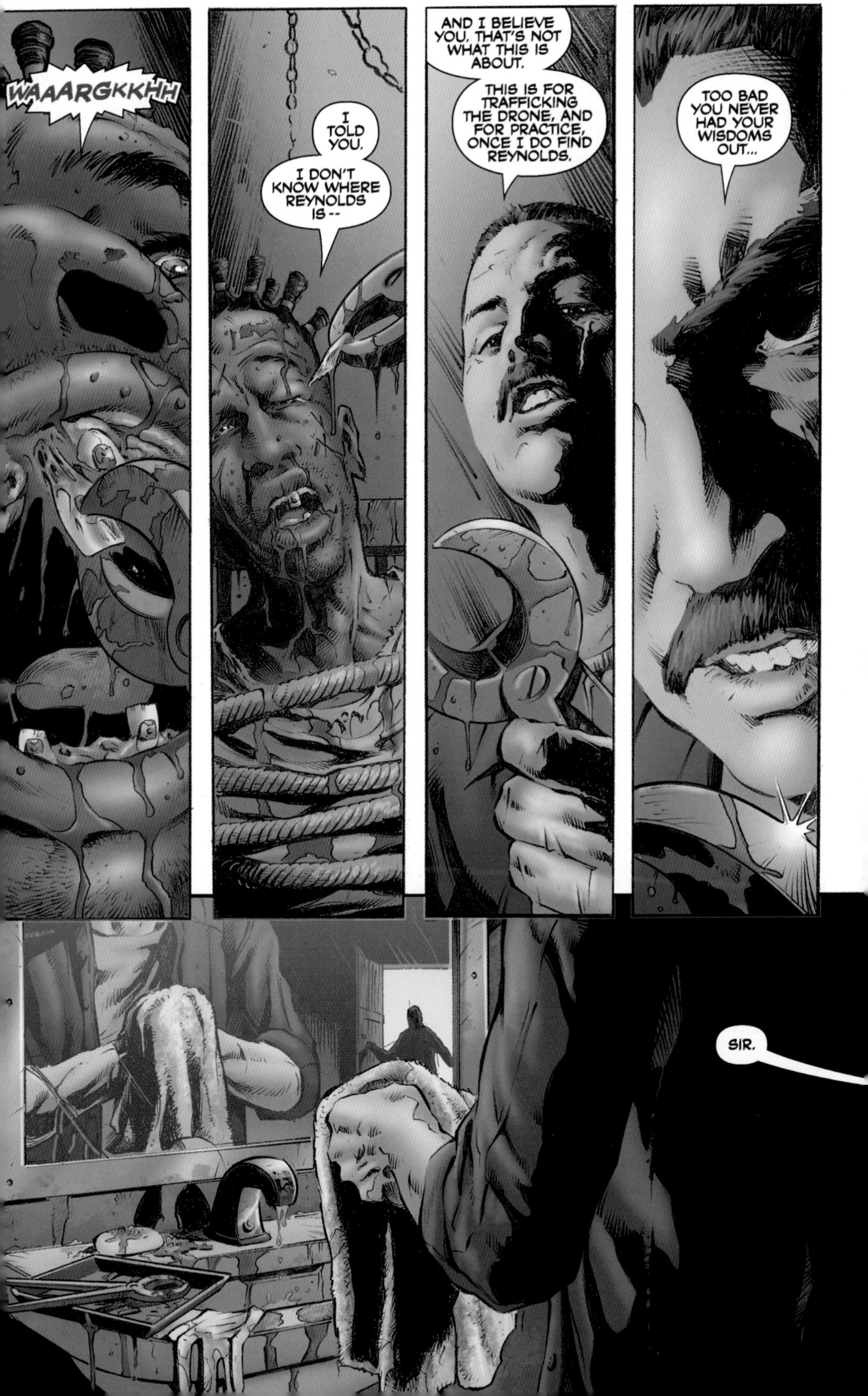
WAAARGKKHH
I TOLD YOU.
I DON'T KNOW WHERE REYNOLDS IS --
AND I BELIEVE YOU. THAT'S NOT WHAT THIS IS ABOUT.
THIS IS FOR TRAFFICKING THE DRONE, AND FOR PRACTICE, ONCE I DO FIND REYNOLDS.
TOO BAD YOU NEVER HAD YOUR WISDOMS OUT...
SIR.

ARE YOU AWARE THE DRONE WAS DESIGNED TO EXPEL MICROSCOPIC TRACKING BEACONS UPON UNEXPECTED SHUTDOWN OR SYSTEM FAILURE?

SIR...

YOU'VE GOT A HIT.

YES. A COUPLE HUNDRED BEACONS MOVING IN UNISON. A SHIP.

MOVEMENT CEASED AT PELORUM, A RESORT WORLD. CARBON SCORING AT THE POINT OF DEPARTURE SUGGESTS--

FIREFLY CLASS?

IT CHECKS.

PELORUM.

YOU'D BETTER BRING YOUR SUNBLOCK, THEN.

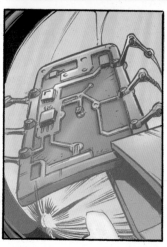

IT'S NOTHIN' FANCY OR ANYTHING.

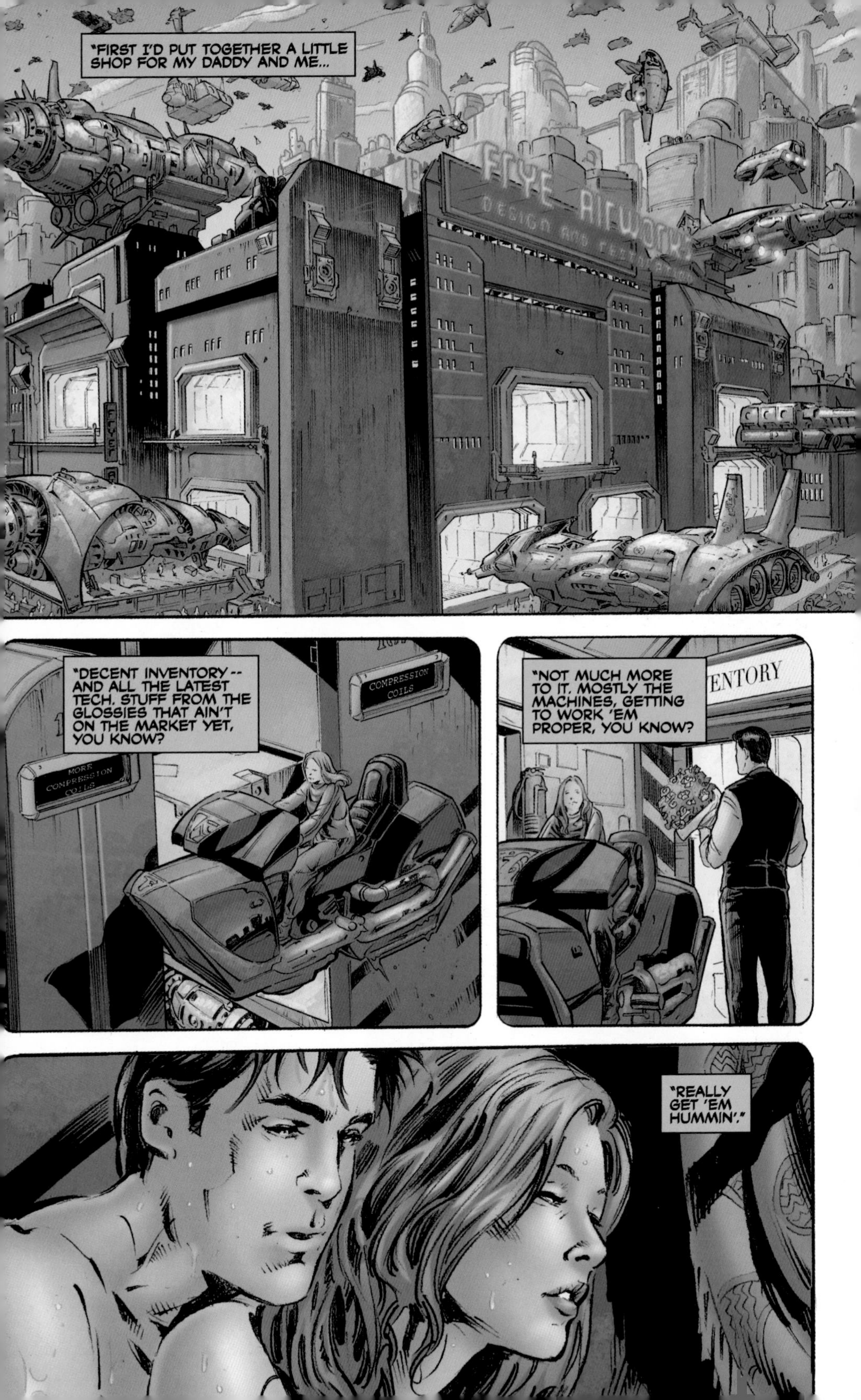
"FIRST I'D PUT TOGETHER A LITTLE SHOP FOR MY DADDY AND ME...
"DECENT INVENTORY--AND ALL THE LATEST TECH. STUFF FROM THE GLOSSIES THAT AIN'T ON THE MARKET YET, YOU KNOW?
COMPRESSION COILS
MORE COMPRESSION COILS
"NOT MUCH MORE TO IT. MOSTLY THE MACHINES, GETTING TO WORK 'EM PROPER, YOU KNOW?
"REALLY GET 'EM HUMMIN'."

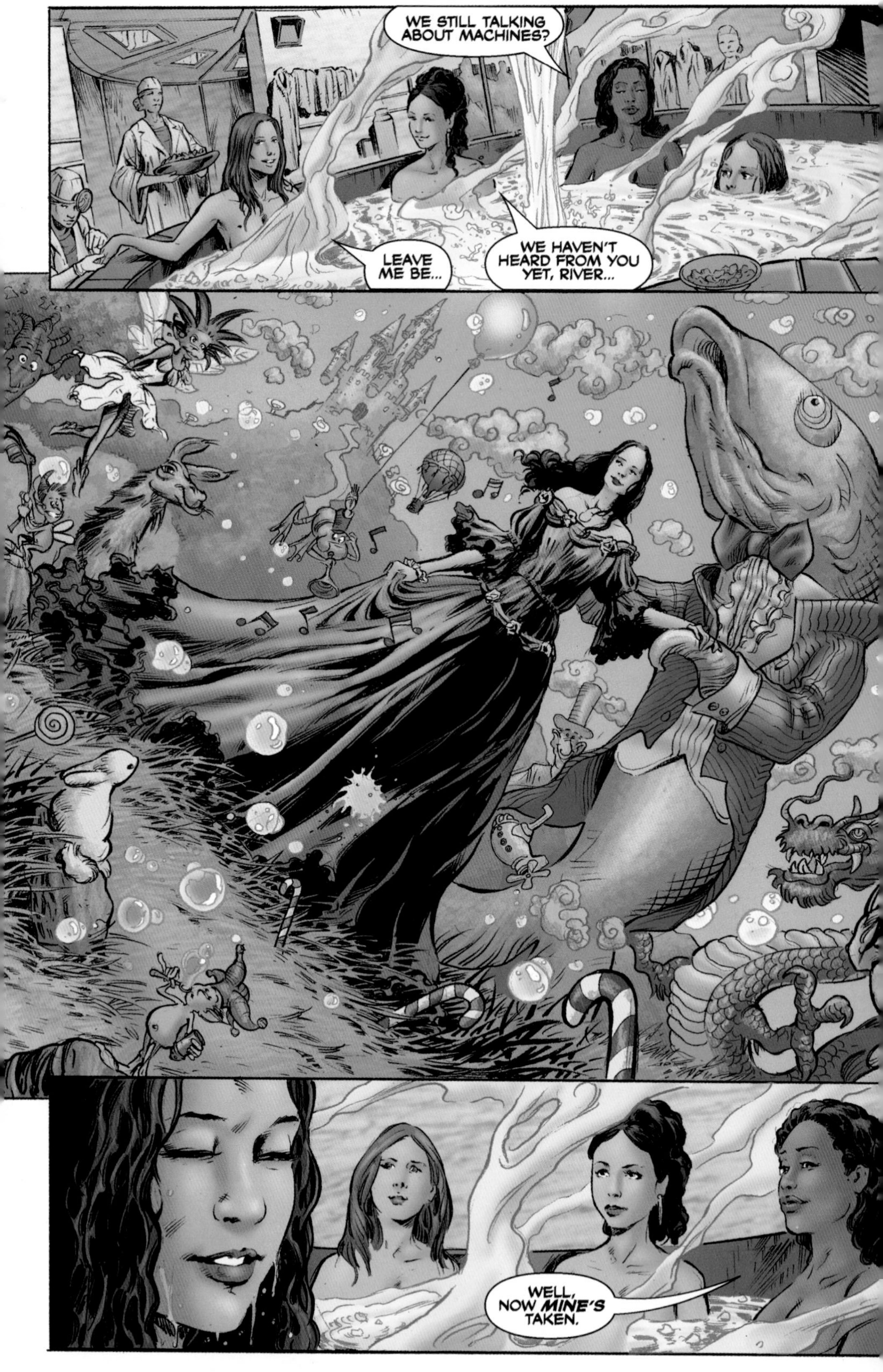
WE STILL TALKING ABOUT MACHINES?
LEAVE ME BE...
WE HAVEN'T HEARD FROM YOU YET, RIVER...
WELL, NOW *MINE'S* TAKEN.

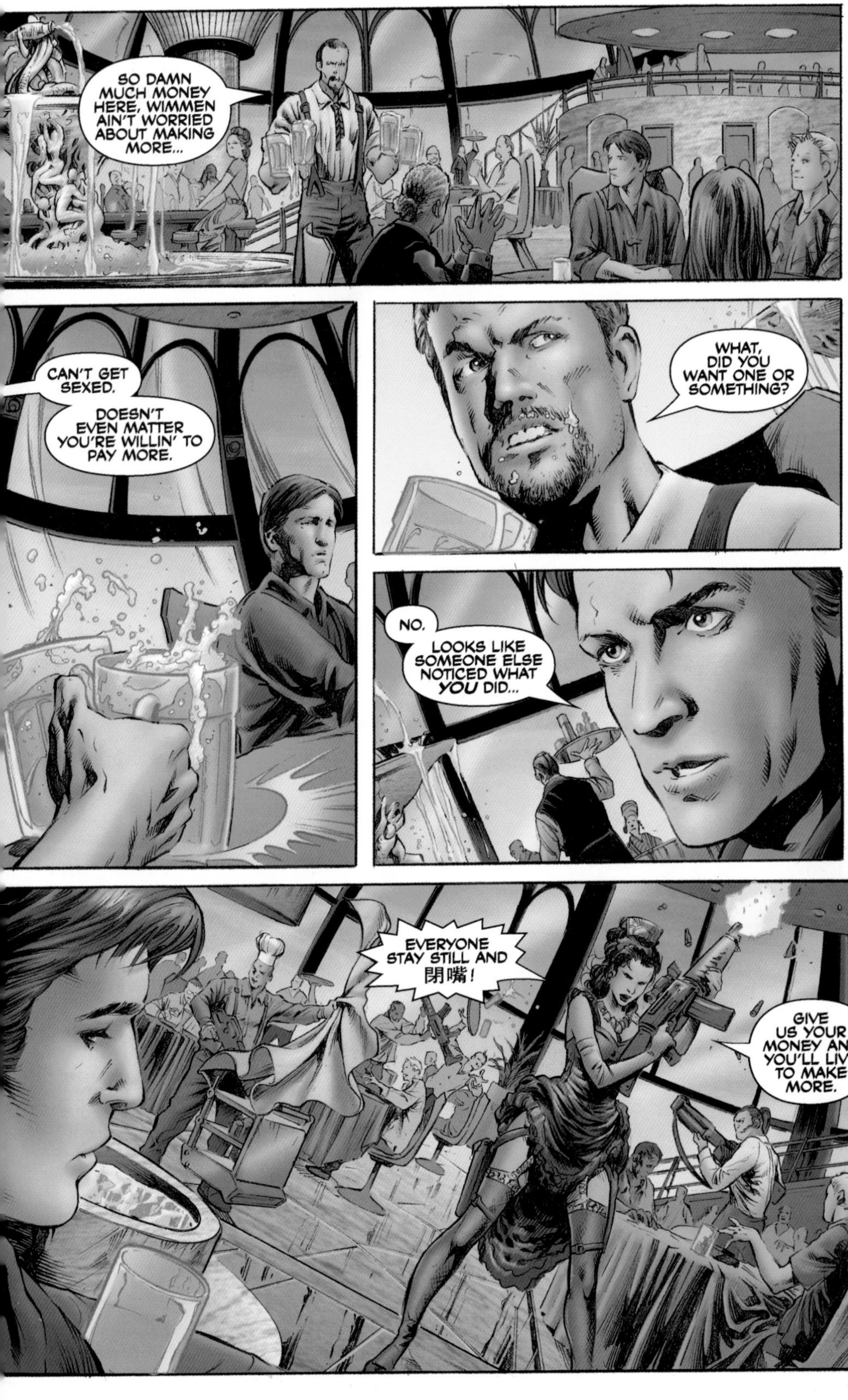
SO DAMN MUCH MONEY HERE, WIMMEN AIN'T WORRIED ABOUT MAKING MORE...
CAN'T GET SEXED.
DOESN'T EVEN MATTER YOU'RE WILLIN' TO PAY MORE.
WHAT, DID YOU WANT ONE OR SOMETHING?
NO.
LOOKS LIKE SOMEONE ELSE NOTICED WHAT *YOU* DID...
EVERYONE STAY STILL AND 閉嘴!
GIVE US YOUR MONEY AND YOU'LL LIVE TO MAKE MORE.

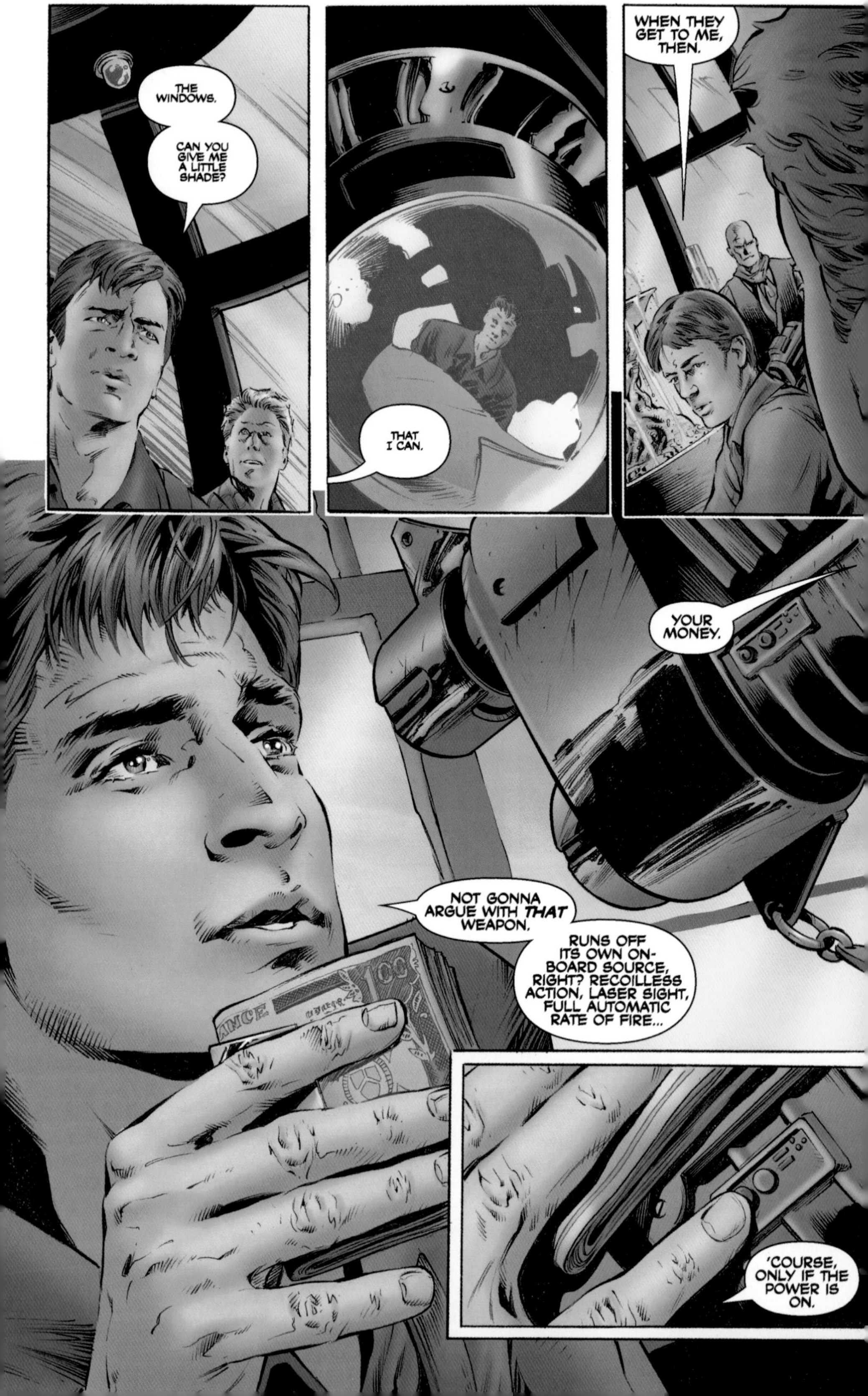
THE WINDOWS.
CAN YOU GIVE ME A LITTLE SHADE?
THAT I CAN.
WHEN THEY GET TO ME, THEN.
YOUR MONEY.
NOT GONNA ARGUE WITH *THAT* WEAPON.
RUNS OFF ITS OWN ON-BOARD SOURCE, RIGHT? RECOILLESS ACTION, LASER SIGHT, FULL AUTOMATIC RATE OF FIRE...
'COURSE, ONLY IF THE POWER IS ON.

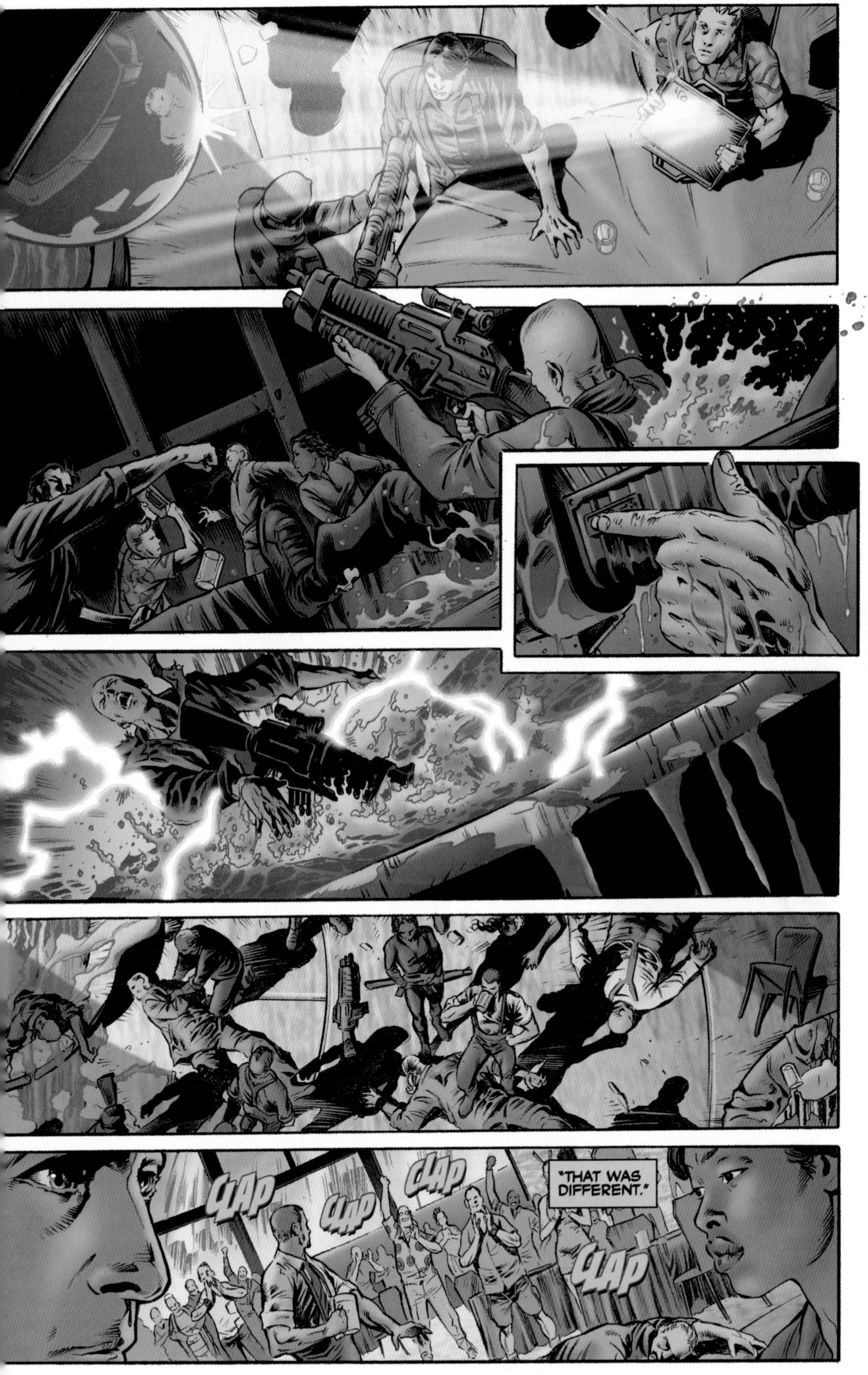
CLAP
CLAP
CLAP
"THAT WAS DIFFERENT."
CLAP

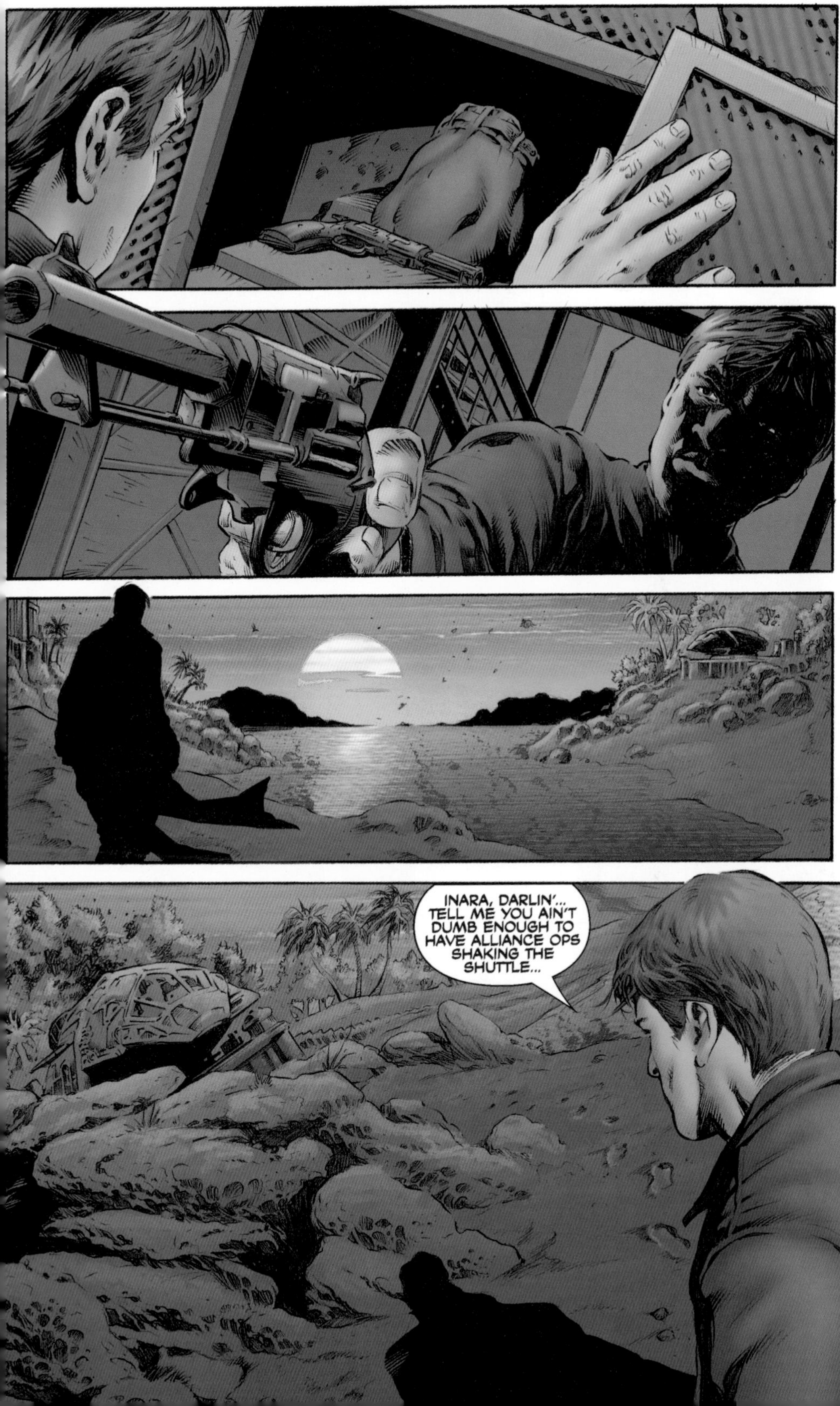
INARA, DARLIN'... TELL ME YOU AIN'T DUMB ENOUGH TO HAVE ALLIANCE OPS SHAKING THE SHUTTLE...

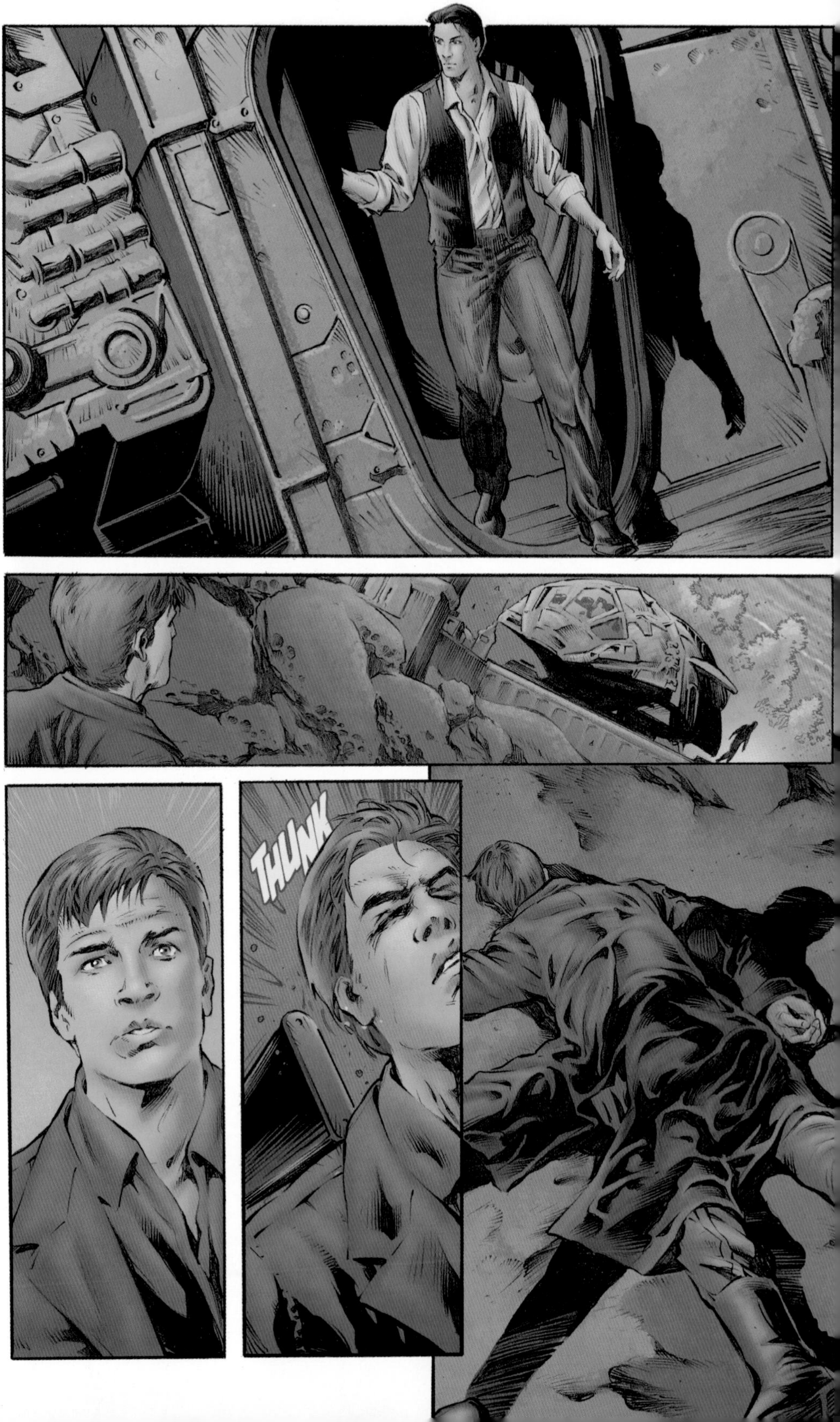
THUNK

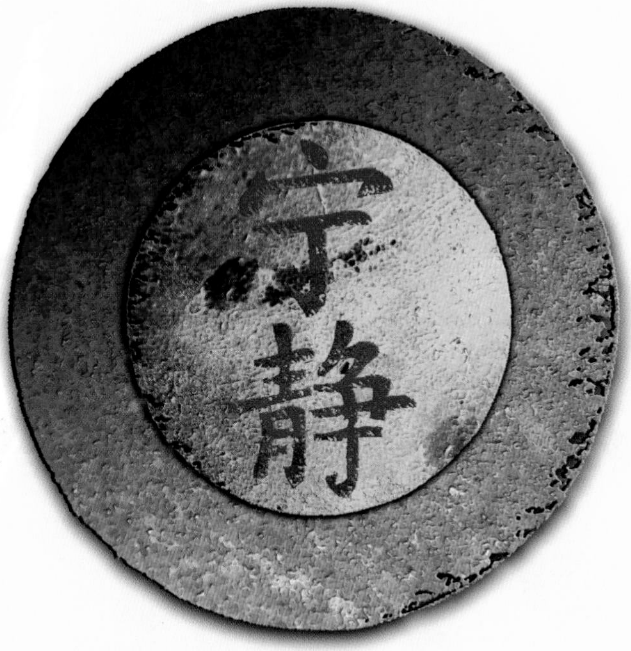
守静

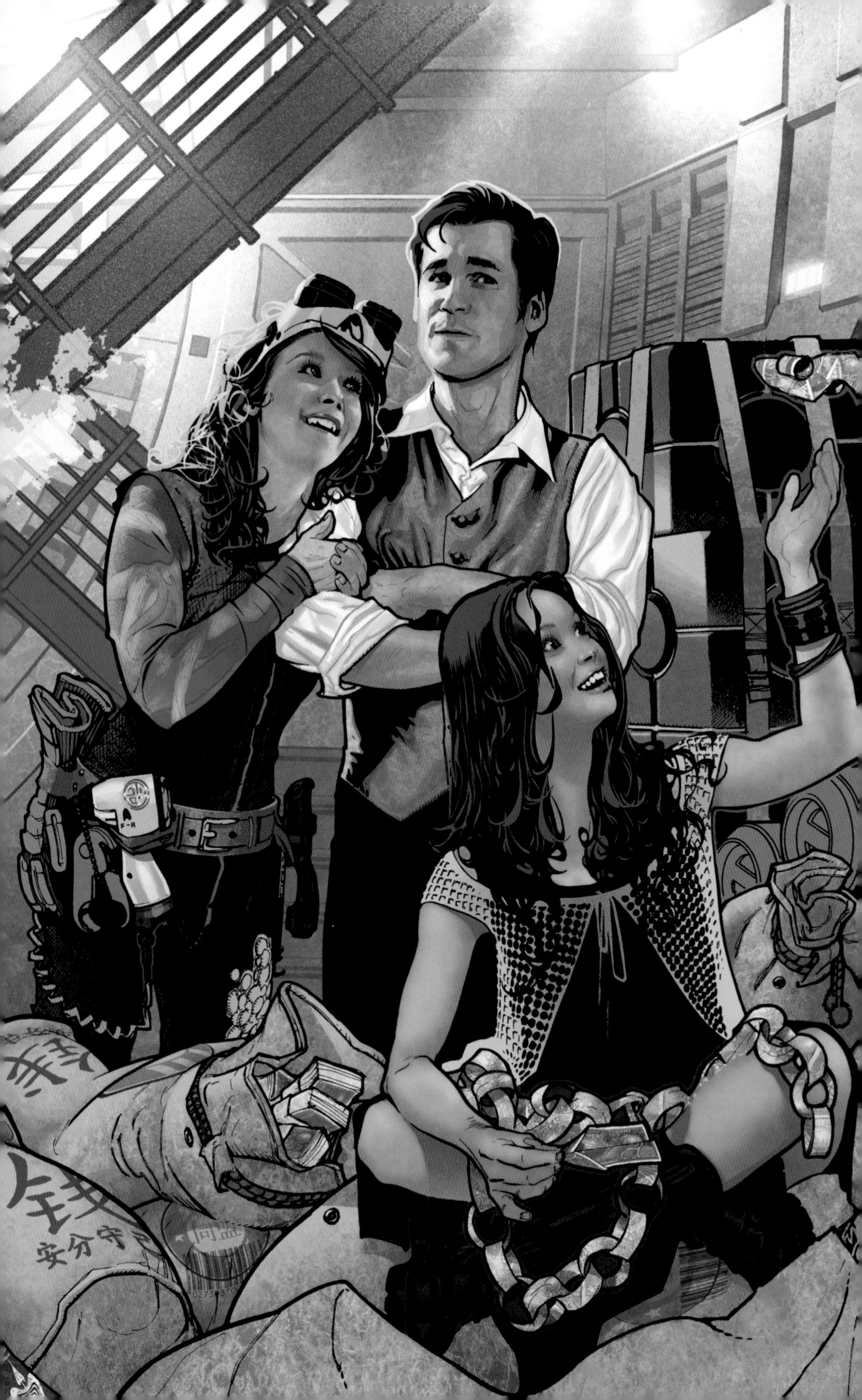
安分守

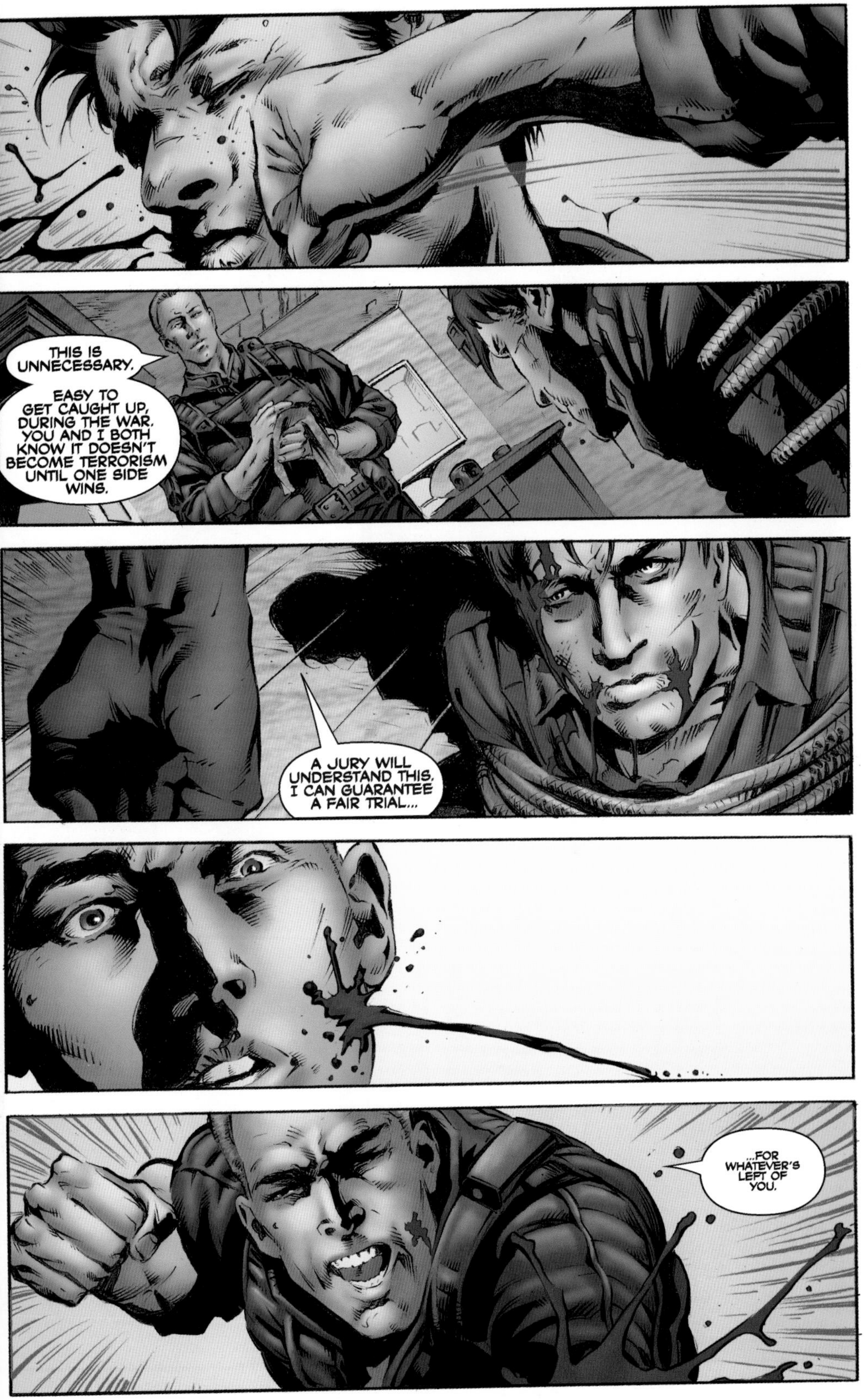
THIS IS UNNECESSARY.
EASY TO GET CAUGHT UP, DURING THE WAR. YOU AND I BOTH KNOW IT DOESN'T BECOME TERRORISM UNTIL ONE SIDE WINS.
A JURY WILL UNDERSTAND THIS. I CAN GUARANTEE A FAIR TRIAL...
...FOR WHATEVER'S LEFT OF YOU.

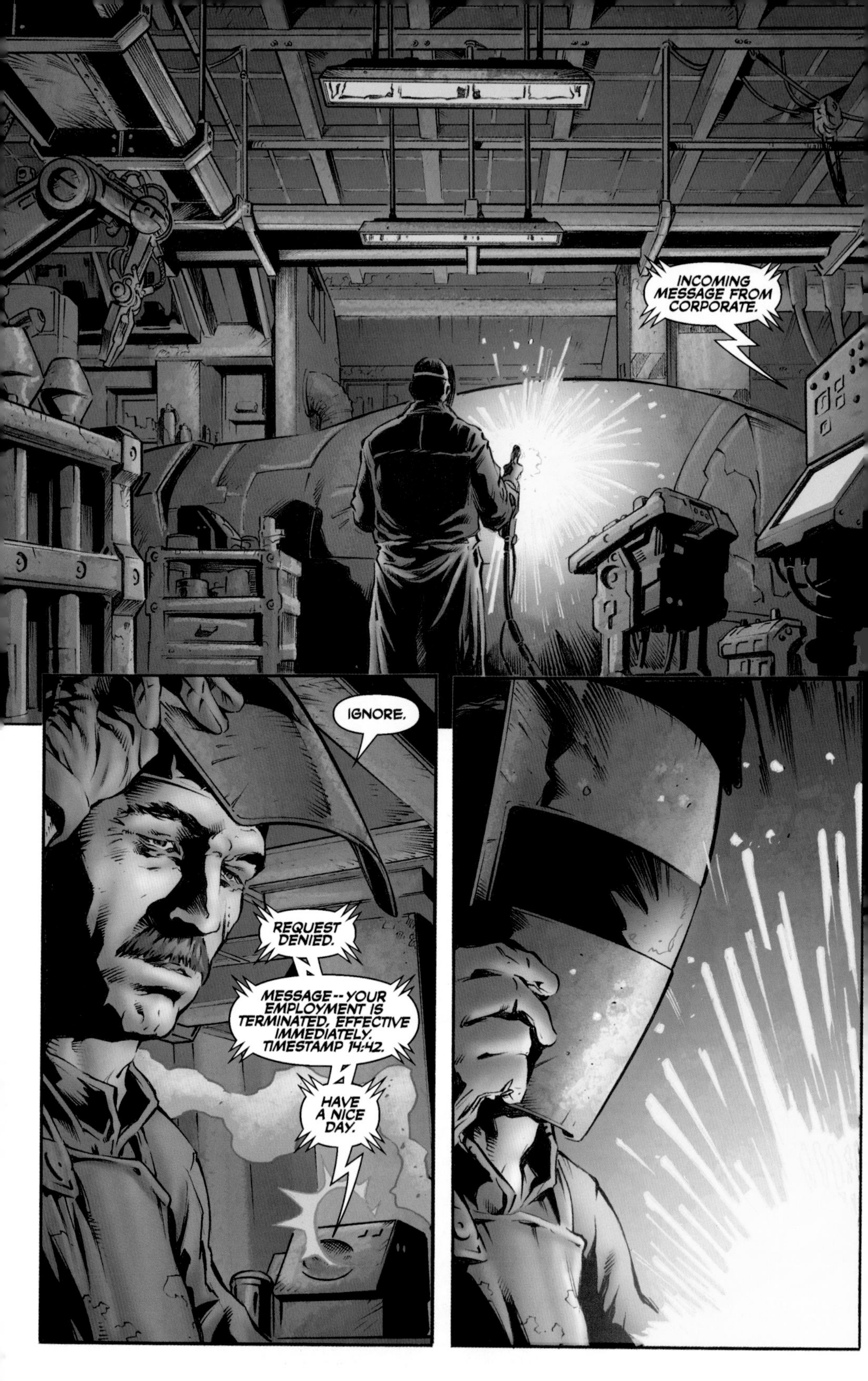
INCOMING MESSAGE FROM CORPORATE.
IGNORE.
REQUEST DENIED.
MESSAGE--YOUR EMPLOYMENT IS TERMINATED, EFFECTIVE IMMEDIATELY. TIMESTAMP 14:42.
HAVE A NICE DAY.

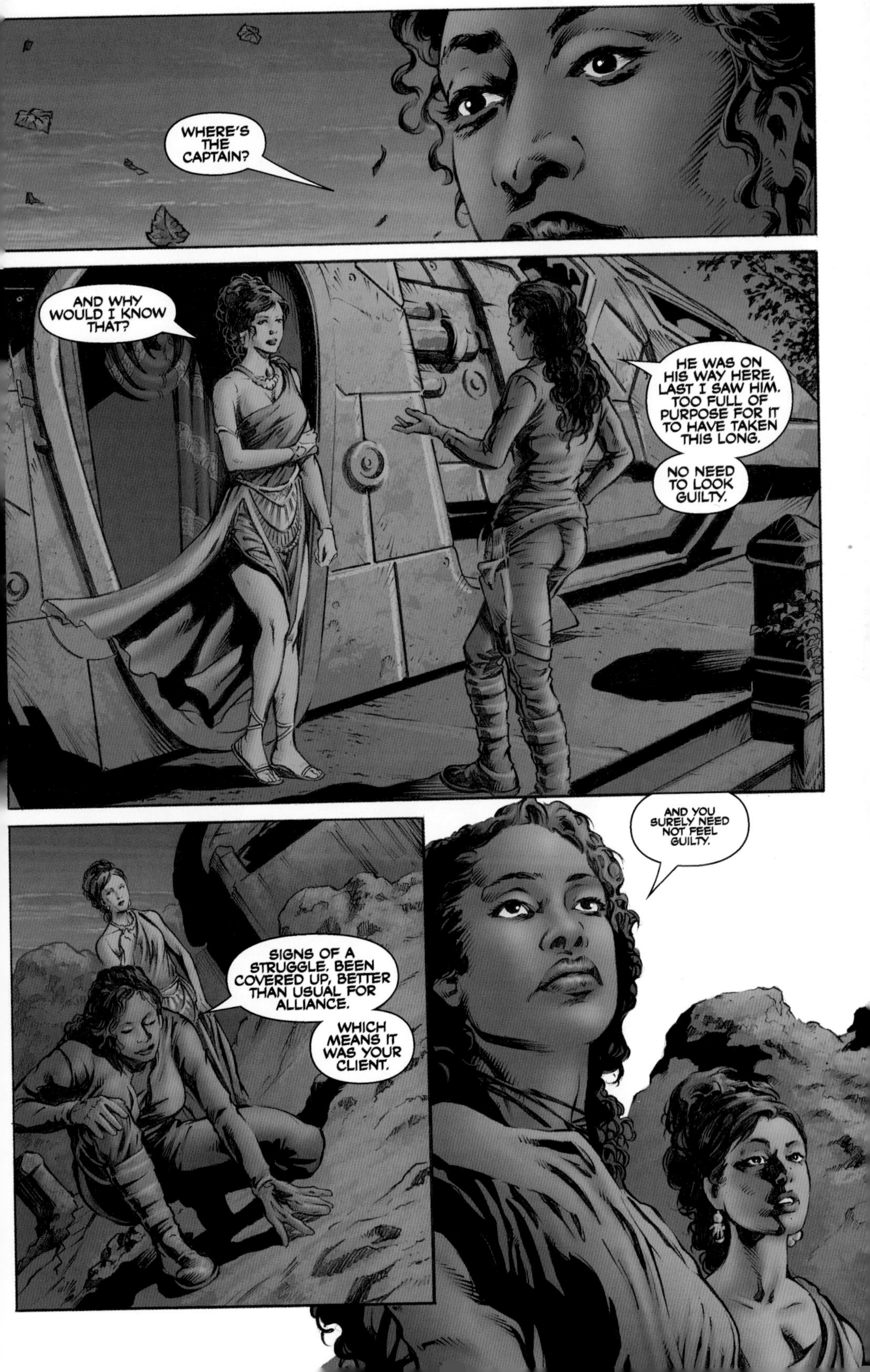
WHERE'S THE CAPTAIN?
AND WHY WOULD I KNOW THAT?
HE WAS ON HIS WAY HERE, LAST I SAW HIM. TOO FULL OF PURPOSE FOR IT TO HAVE TAKEN THIS LONG.
NO NEED TO LOOK GUILTY.
SIGNS OF A STRUGGLE. BEEN COVERED UP, BETTER THAN USUAL FOR ALLIANCE.
WHICH MEANS IT WAS YOUR CLIENT.
AND YOU SURELY NEED NOT FEEL GUILTY.

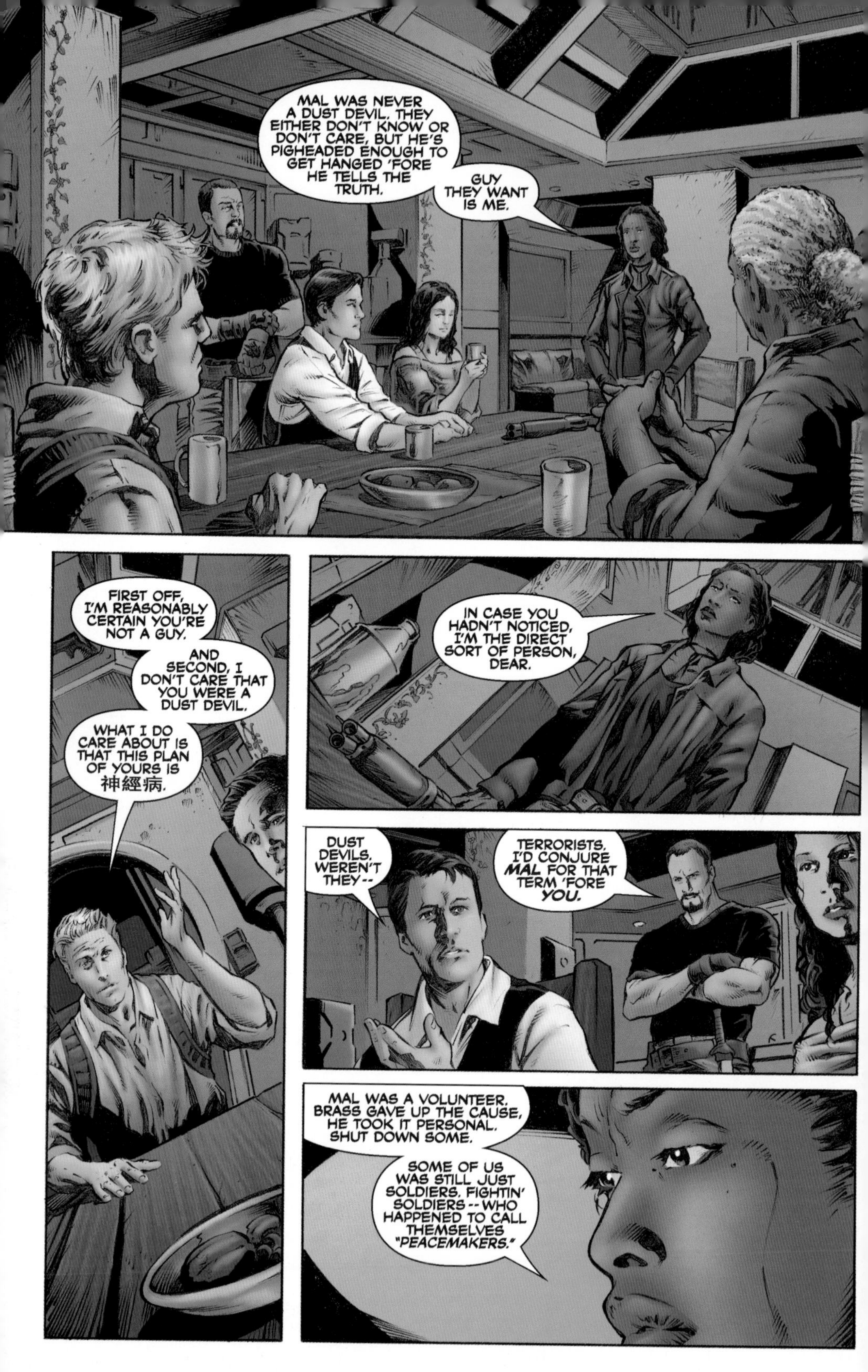
MAL WAS NEVER A DUST DEVIL. THEY EITHER DON'T KNOW OR DON'T CARE, BUT HE'S PIGHEADED ENOUGH TO GET HANGED 'FORE HE TELLS THE TRUTH.
GUY THEY WANT IS ME.
FIRST OFF, I'M REASONABLY CERTAIN YOU'RE NOT A GUY.
AND SECOND, I DON'T CARE THAT YOU WERE A DUST DEVIL.
WHAT I DO CARE ABOUT IS THAT THIS PLAN OF YOURS IS 神經病.
IN CASE YOU HADN'T NOTICED, I'M THE DIRECT SORT OF PERSON, DEAR.
DUST DEVILS. WEREN'T THEY--
TERRORISTS. I'D CONJURE *MAL* FOR THAT TERM 'FORE *YOU.*
MAL WAS A VOLUNTEER. BRASS GAVE UP THE CAUSE, HE TOOK IT PERSONAL. SHUT DOWN SOME.
SOME OF US WAS STILL JUST SOLDIERS. FIGHTIN' SOLDIERS--WHO HAPPENED TO CALL THEMSELVES *"PEACEMAKERS."*

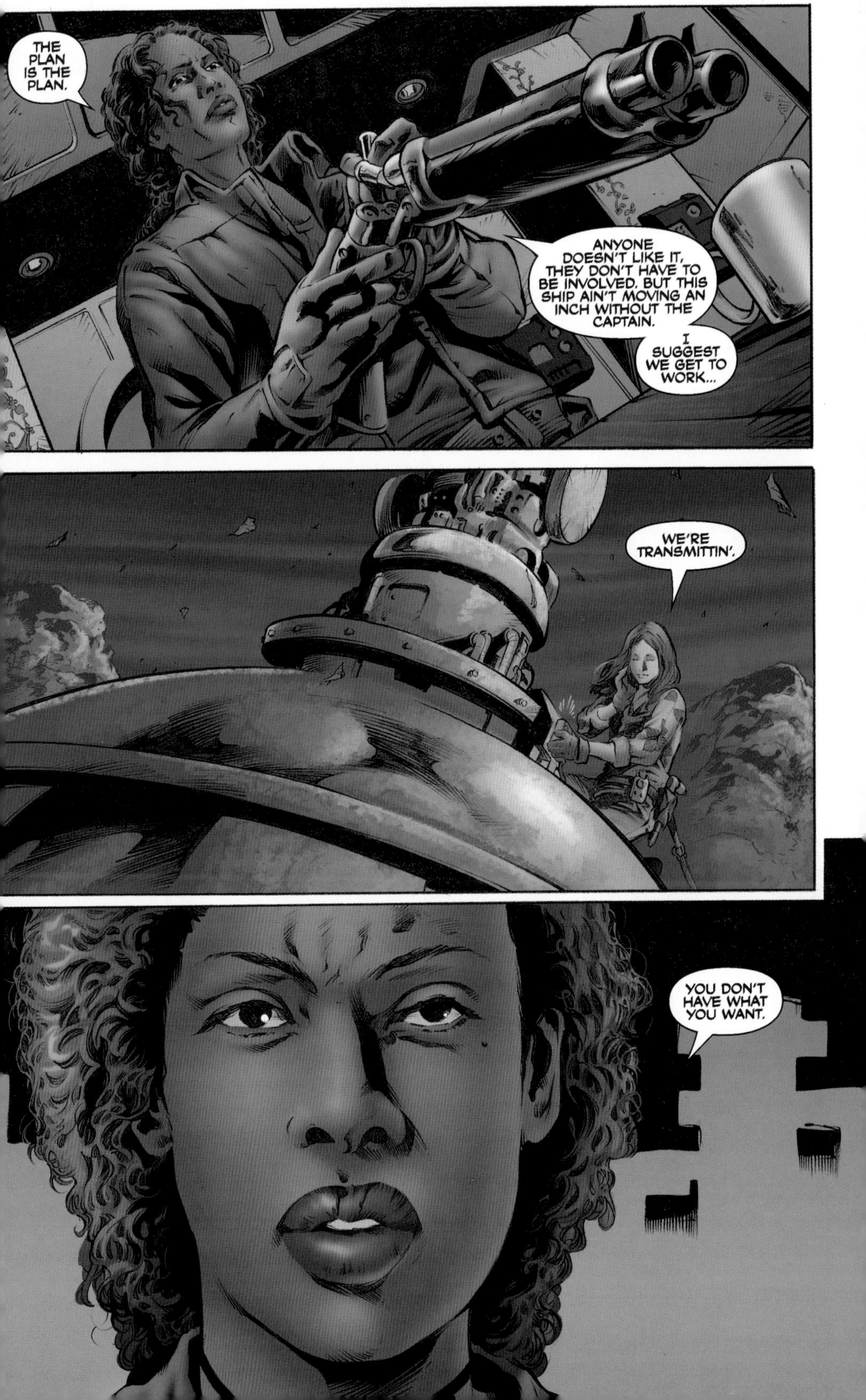
THE PLAN IS THE PLAN.
ANYONE DOESN'T LIKE IT, THEY DON'T HAVE TO BE INVOLVED, BUT THIS SHIP AIN'T MOVING AN INCH WITHOUT THE CAPTAIN.
I SUGGEST WE GET TO WORK...
WE'RE TRANSMITTIN'.
YOU DON'T HAVE WHAT YOU WANT.

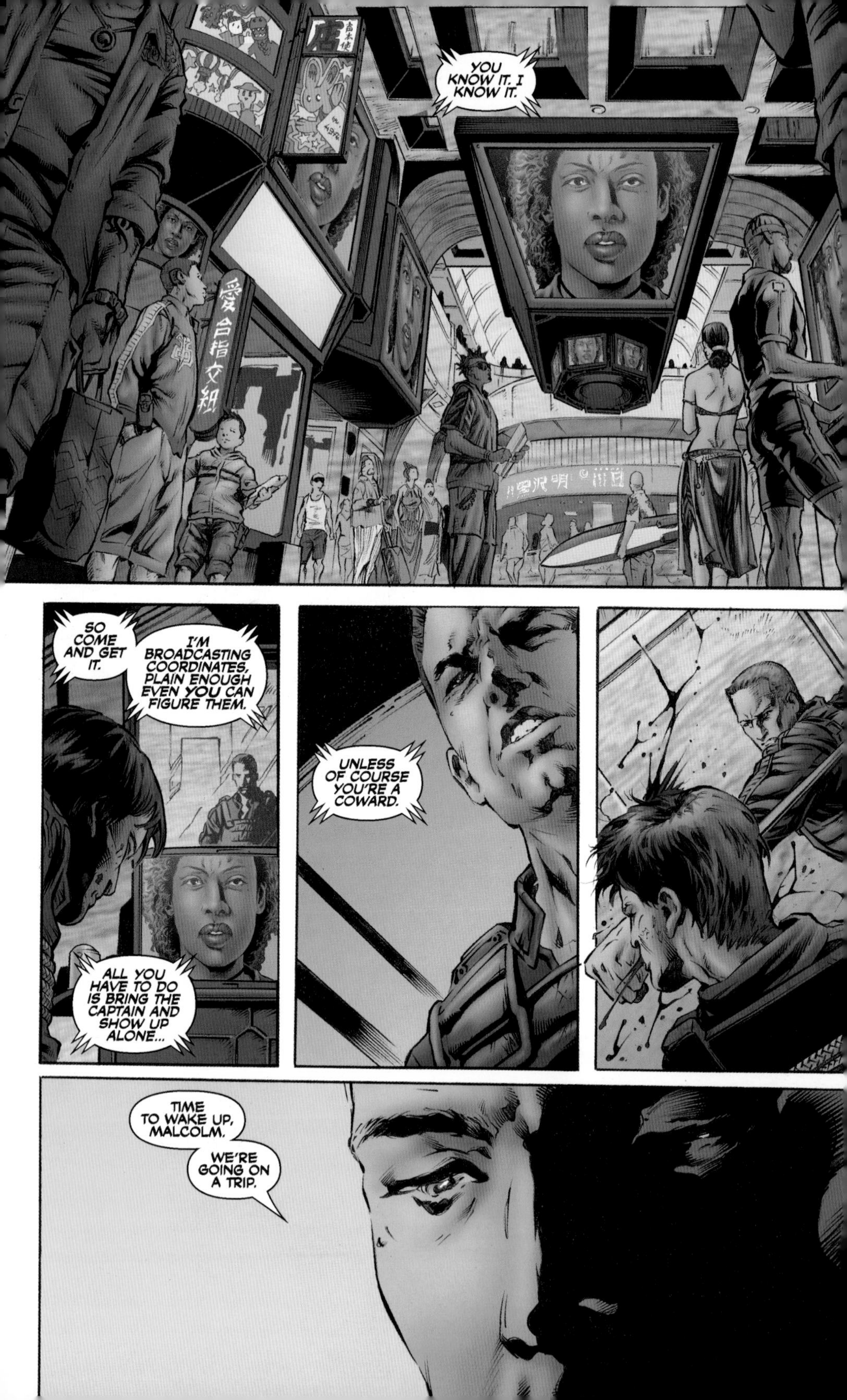
YOU KNOW IT. I KNOW IT.
SO COME AND GET IT.
I'M BROADCASTING COORDINATES, PLAIN ENOUGH EVEN YOU CAN FIGURE THEM.
ALL YOU HAVE TO DO IS BRING THE CAPTAIN AND SHOW UP ALONE...
UNLESS OF COURSE YOU'RE A COWARD.
TIME TO WAKE UP, MALCOLM.
WE'RE GOING ON A TRIP.

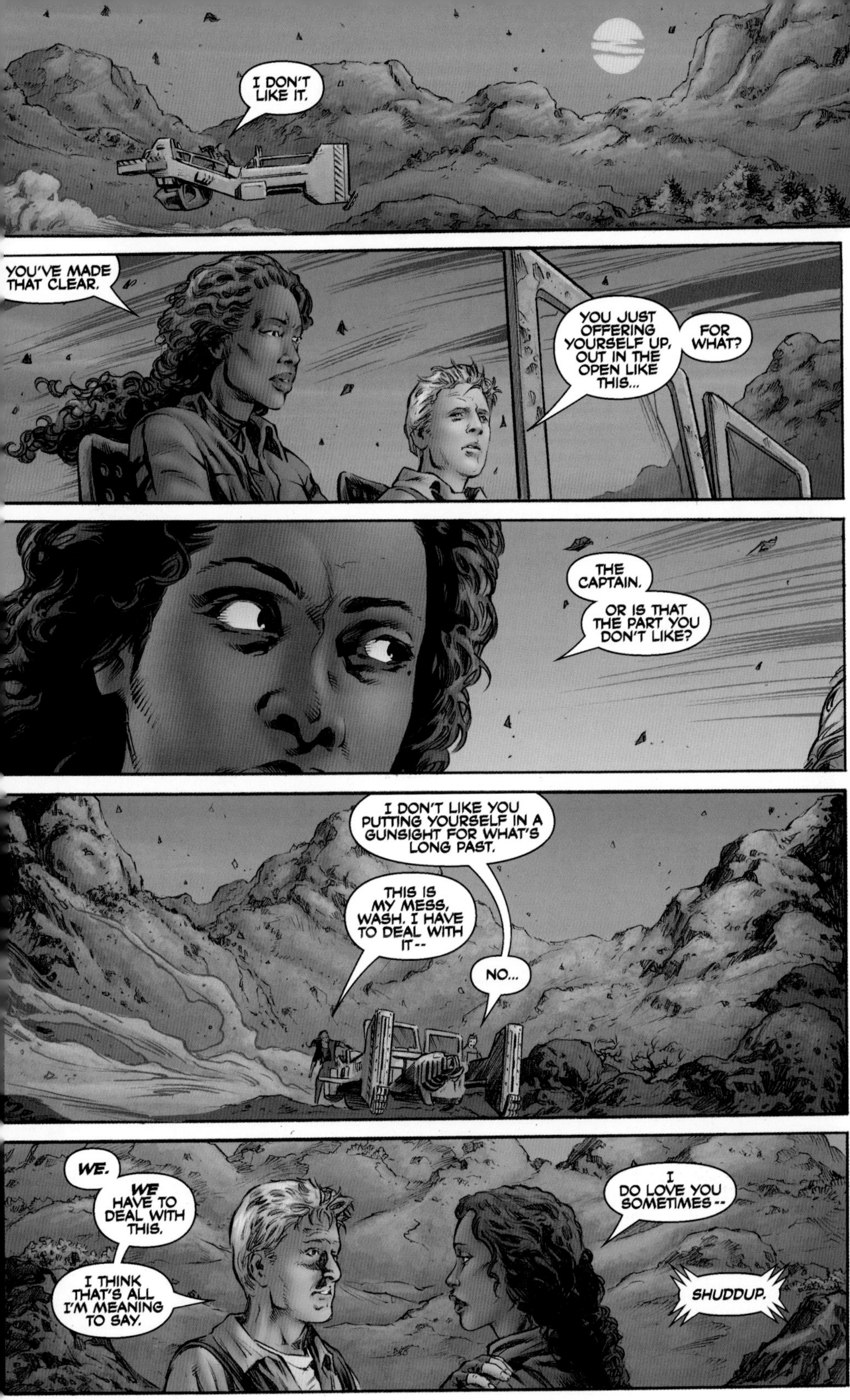
I DON'T LIKE IT.
YOU'VE MADE THAT CLEAR.
YOU JUST OFFERING YOURSELF UP, OUT IN THE OPEN LIKE THIS...
FOR WHAT?
THE CAPTAIN.
OR IS THAT THE PART YOU DON'T LIKE?
I DON'T LIKE YOU PUTTING YOURSELF IN A GUNSIGHT FOR WHAT'S LONG PAST.
THIS IS MY MESS, WASH. I HAVE TO DEAL WITH IT --
NO...
WE.
WE HAVE TO DEAL WITH THIS.
I THINK THAT'S ALL I'M MEANING TO SAY.
I DO LOVE YOU SOMETIMES --
SHUDDUP.

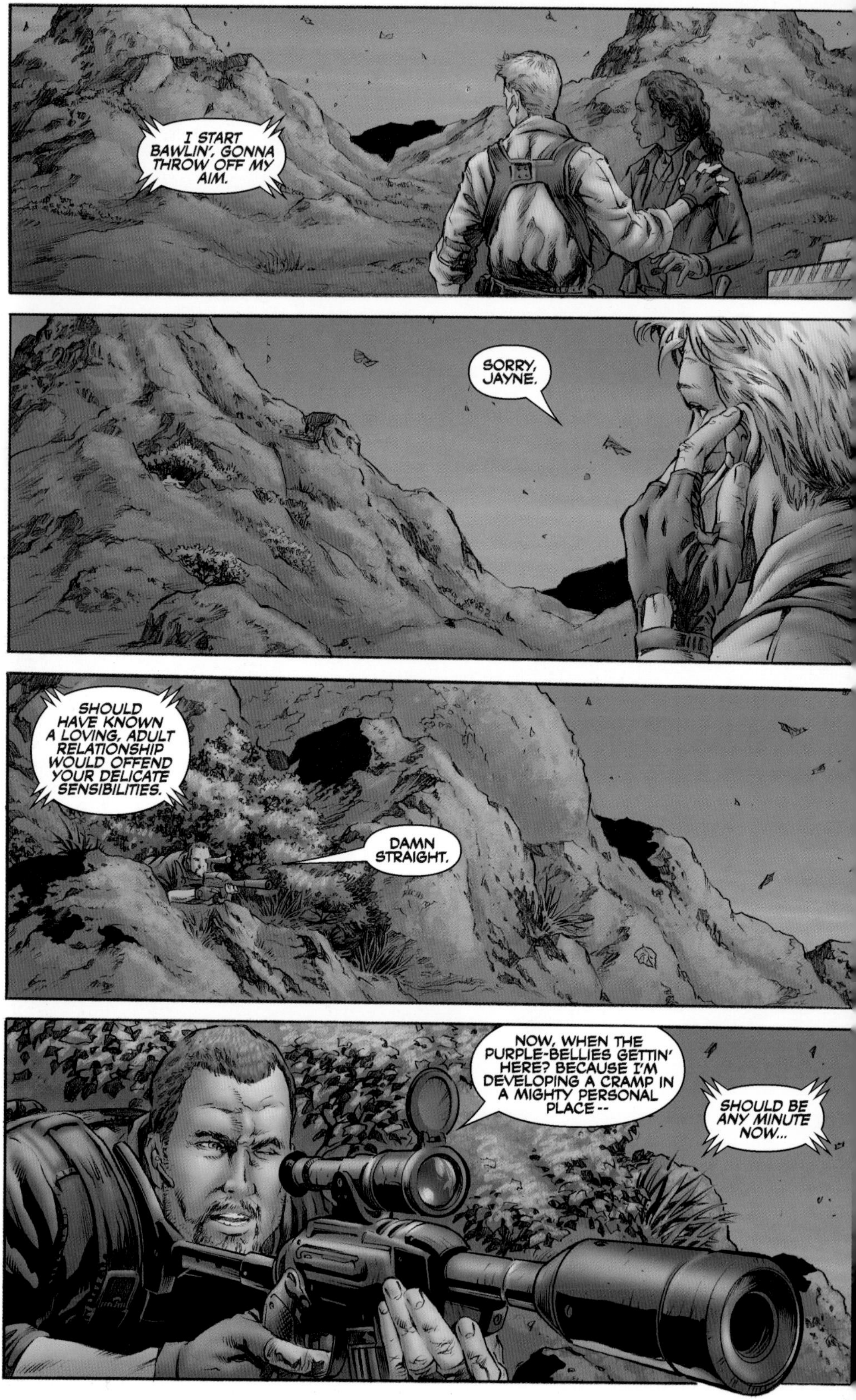
I START BAWLIN', GONNA THROW OFF MY AIM.
SORRY, JAYNE.
SHOULD HAVE KNOWN A LOVING, ADULT RELATIONSHIP WOULD OFFEND YOUR DELICATE SENSIBILITIES.
DAMN STRAIGHT.
NOW, WHEN THE PURPLE-BELLIES GETTIN' HERE? BECAUSE I'M DEVELOPING A CRAMP IN A MIGHTY PERSONAL PLACE --
SHOULD BE ANY MINUTE NOW...

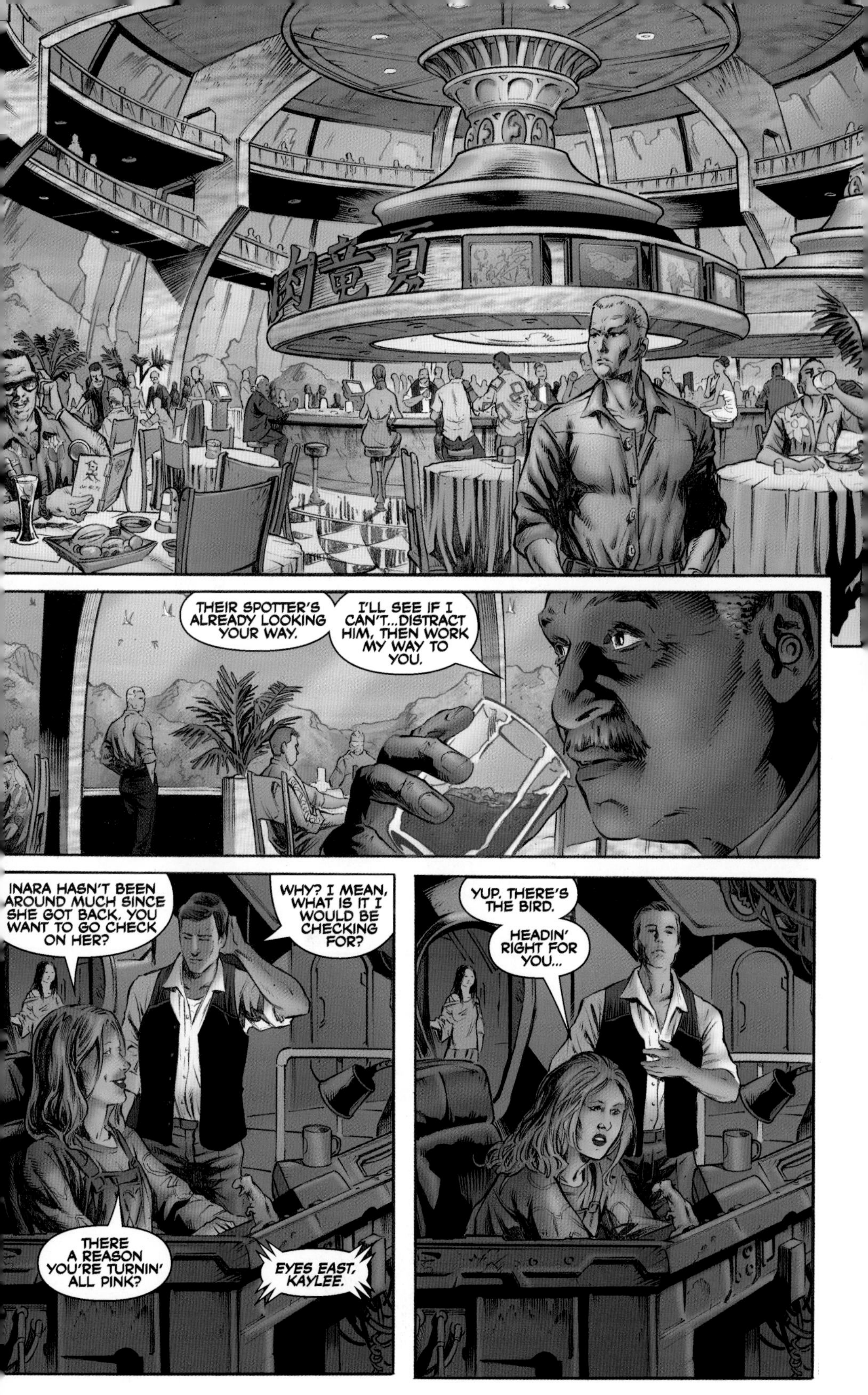
THEIR SPOTTER'S ALREADY LOOKING YOUR WAY.
I'LL SEE IF I CAN'T...DISTRACT HIM, THEN WORK MY WAY TO YOU.
INARA HASN'T BEEN AROUND MUCH SINCE SHE GOT BACK. YOU WANT TO GO CHECK ON HER?
WHY? I MEAN, WHAT IS IT I WOULD BE CHECKING FOR?
THERE A REASON YOU'RE TURNIN' ALL PINK?
EYES EAST, KAYLEE.
YUP, THERE'S THE BIRD.
HEADIN' RIGHT FOR YOU...

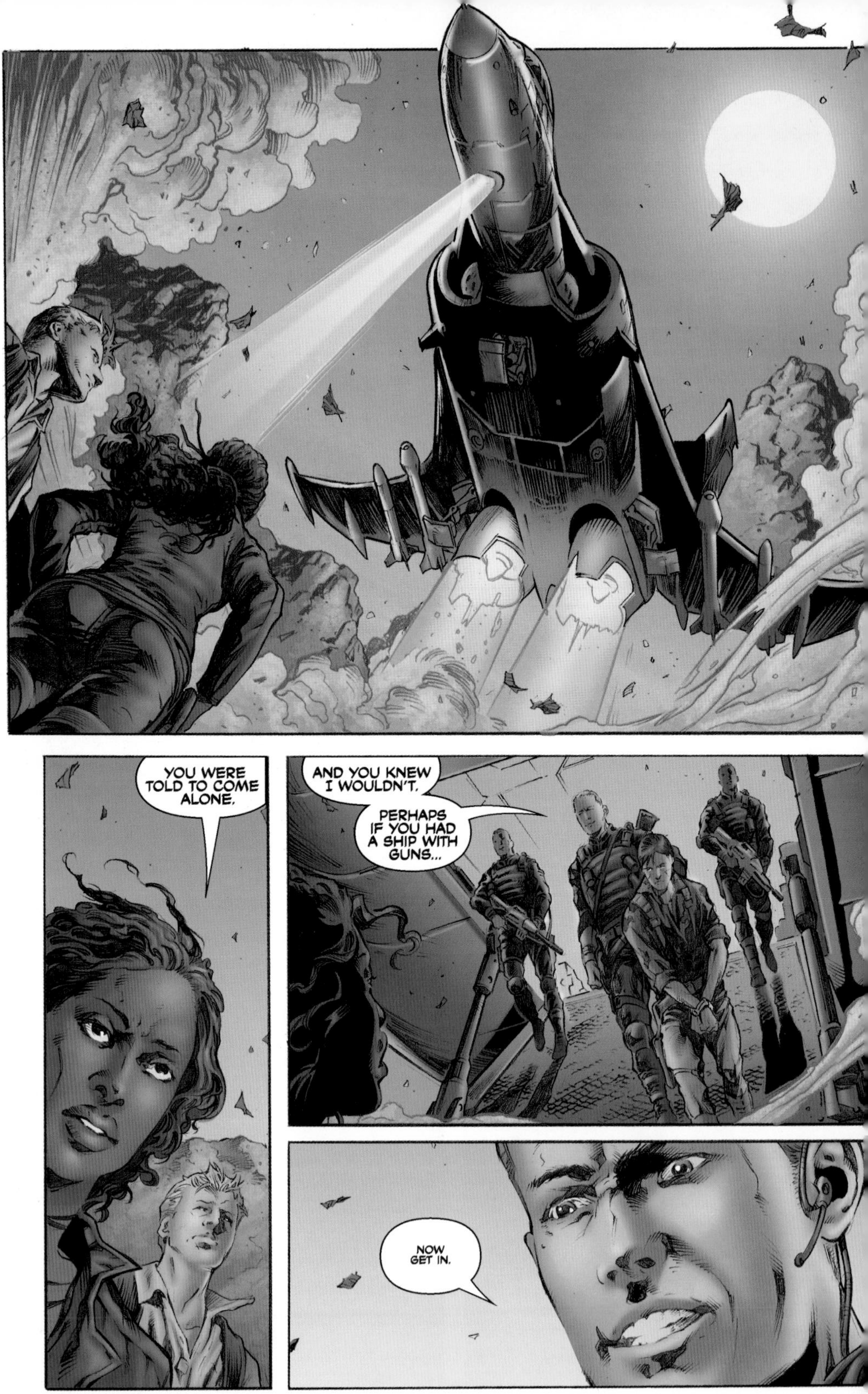
YOU WERE TOLD TO COME ALONE.
AND YOU KNEW I WOULDN'T.
PERHAPS IF YOU HAD A SHIP WITH GUNS...
NOW GET IN.

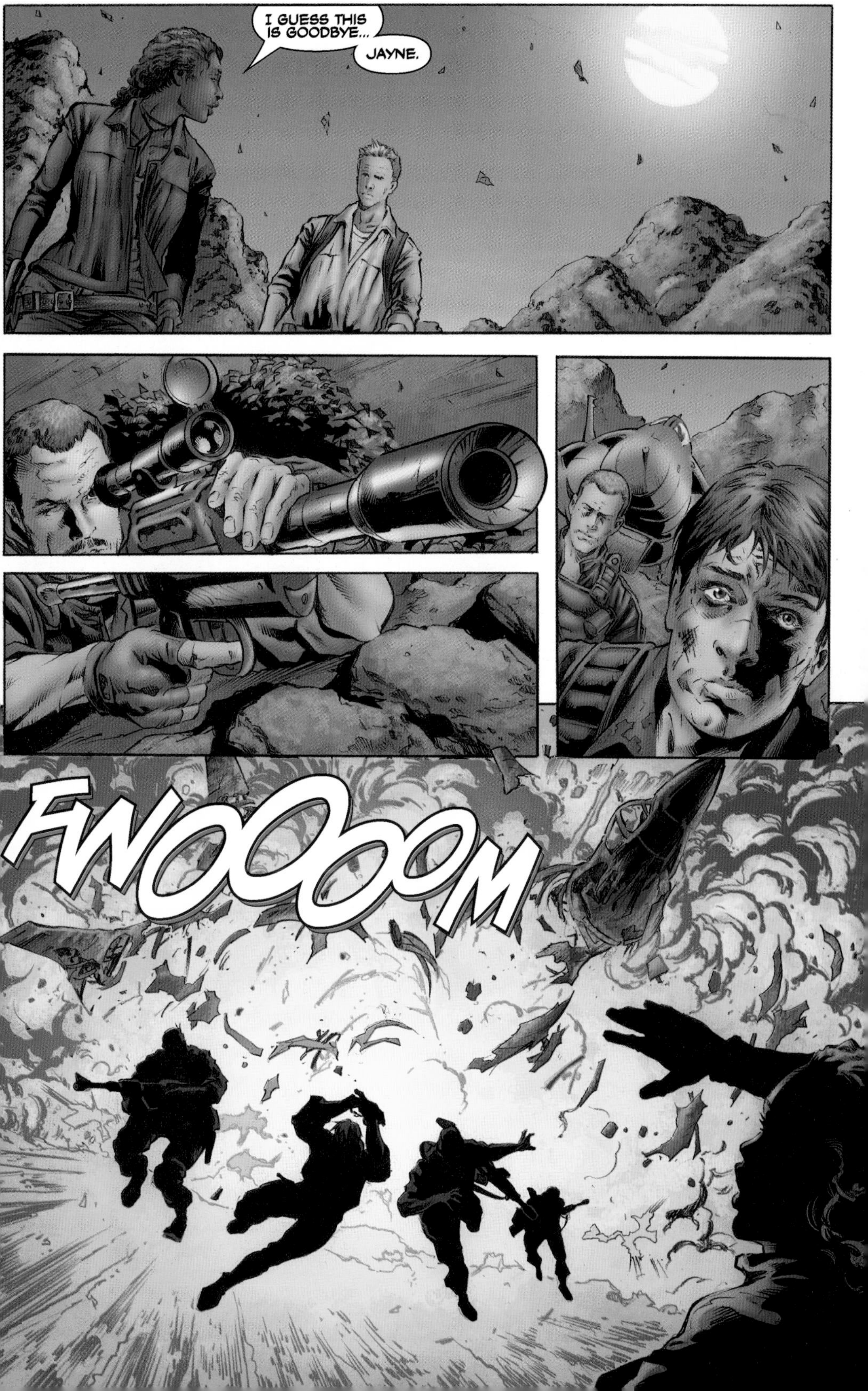
I GUESS THIS IS GOODBYE...
JAYNE.
FWOOOOM

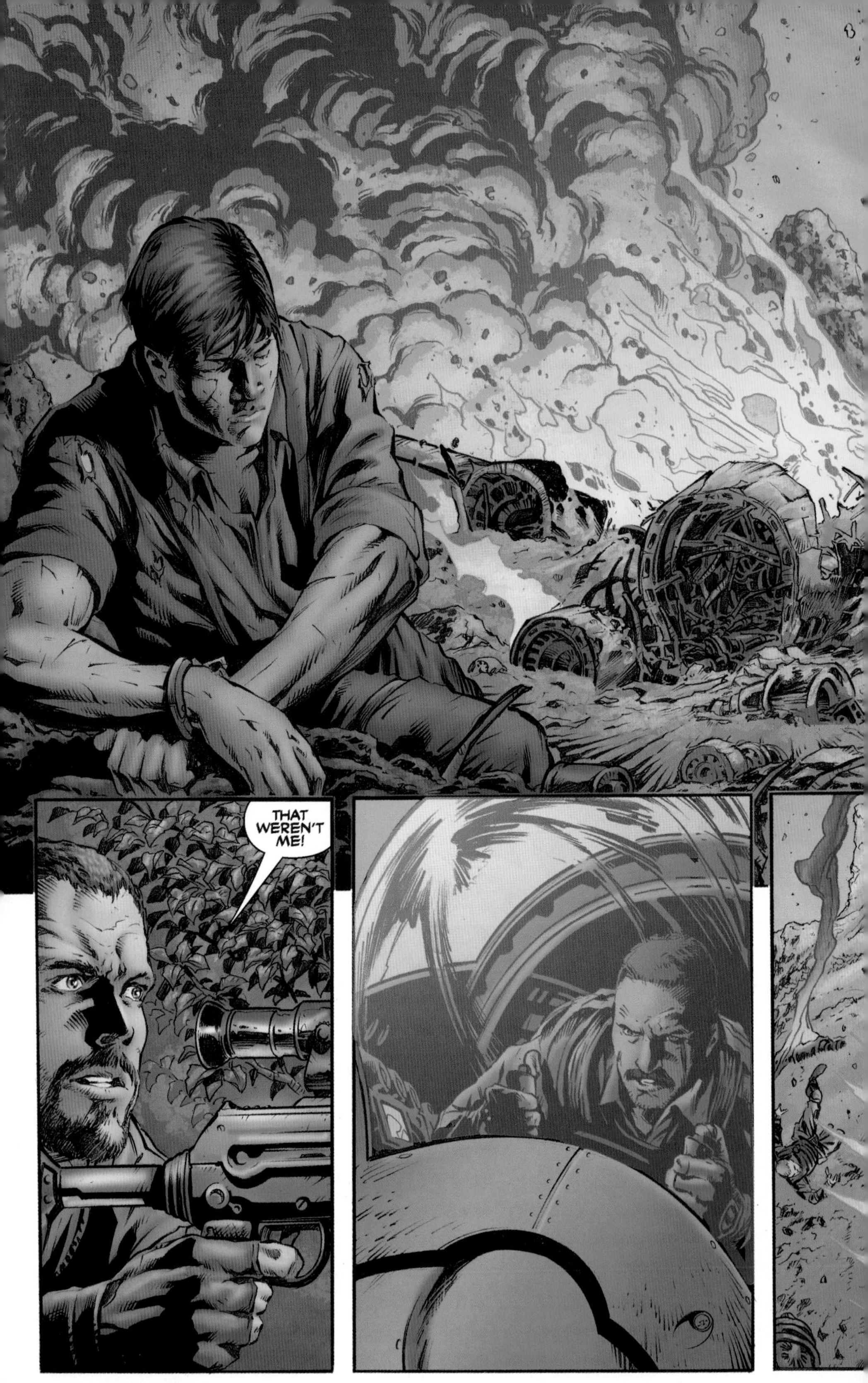
THAT WEREN'T ME!

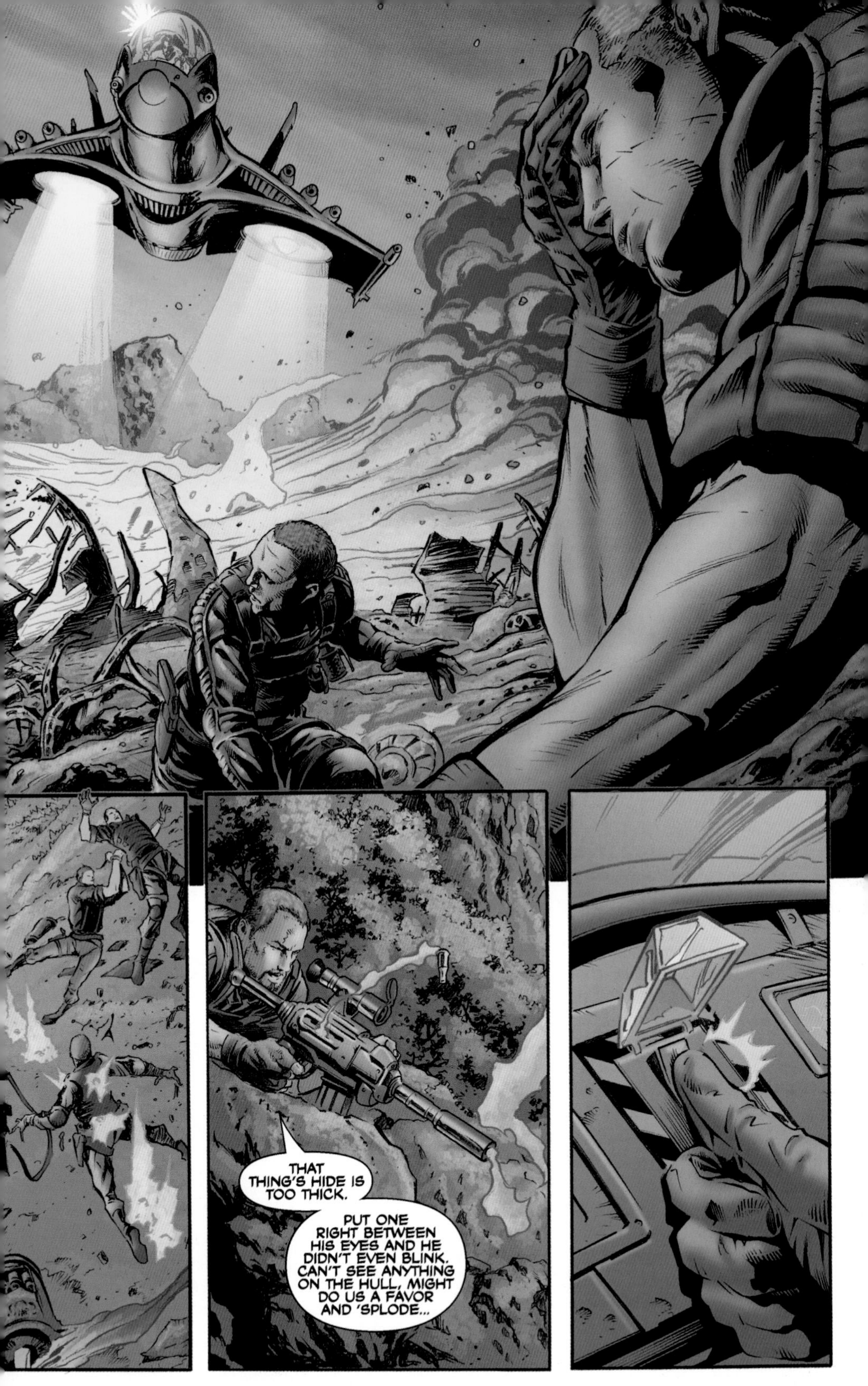
THAT THING'S HIDE IS TOO THICK.
PUT ONE RIGHT BETWEEN HIS EYES AND HE DIDN'T EVEN BLINK. CAN'T SEE ANYTHING ON THE HULL, MIGHT DO US A FAVOR AND 'SPLODE...

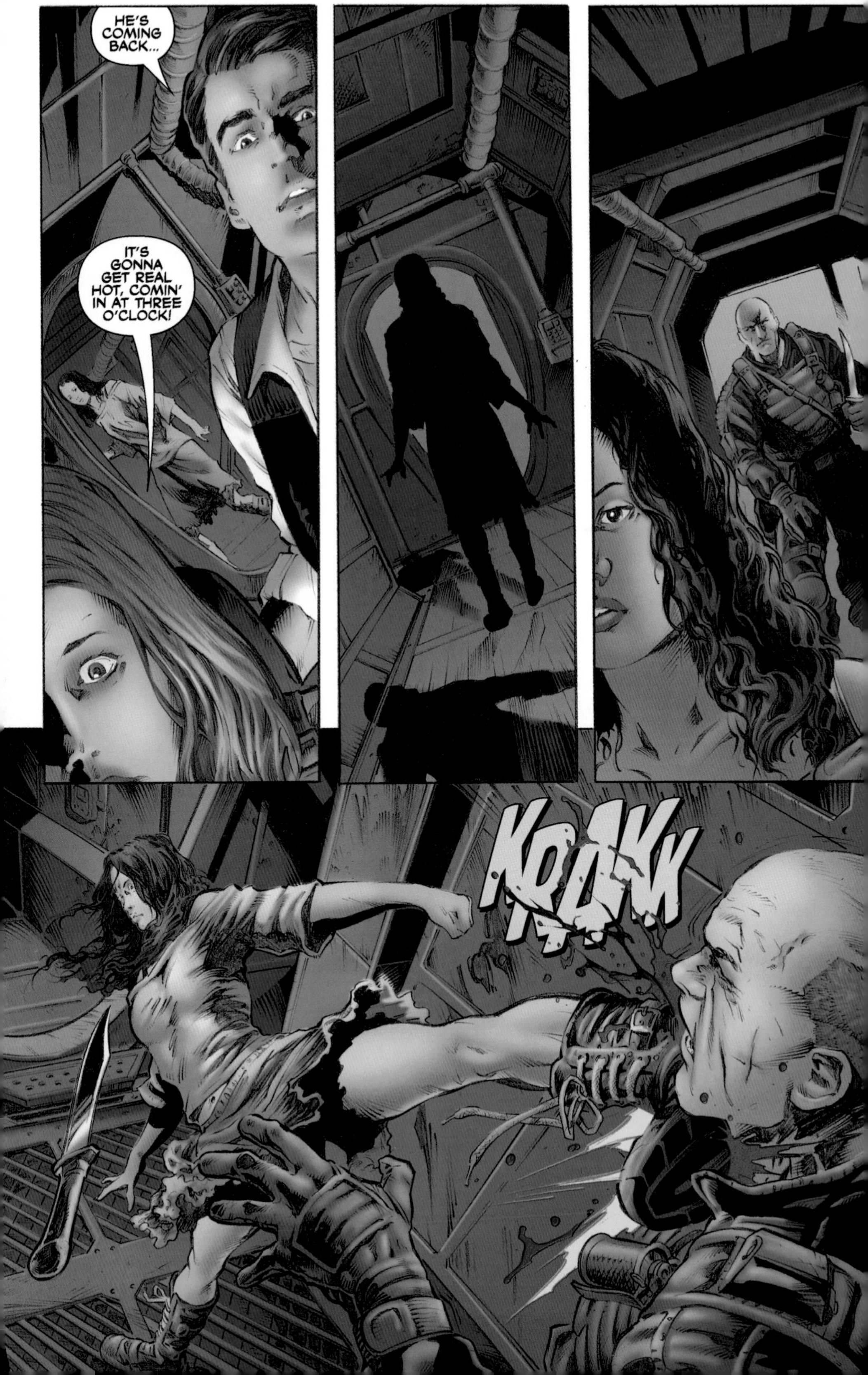
HE'S COMING BACK...
IT'S GONNA GET REAL HOT, COMIN' IN AT THREE O'CLOCK!
KRAKK

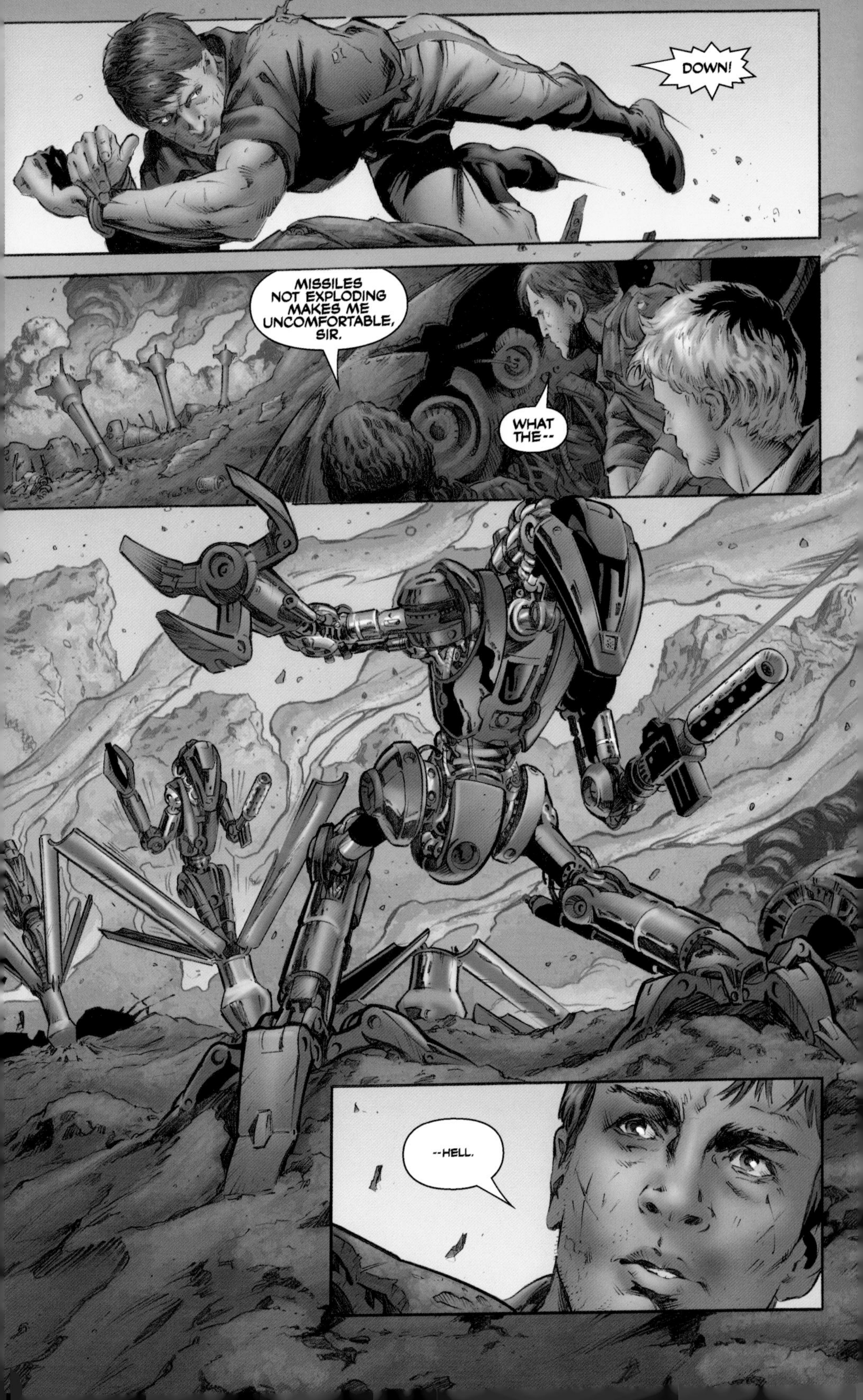
DOWN!
MISSILES NOT EXPLODING MAKES ME UNCOMFORTABLE, SIR.
WHAT THE--
--HELL.

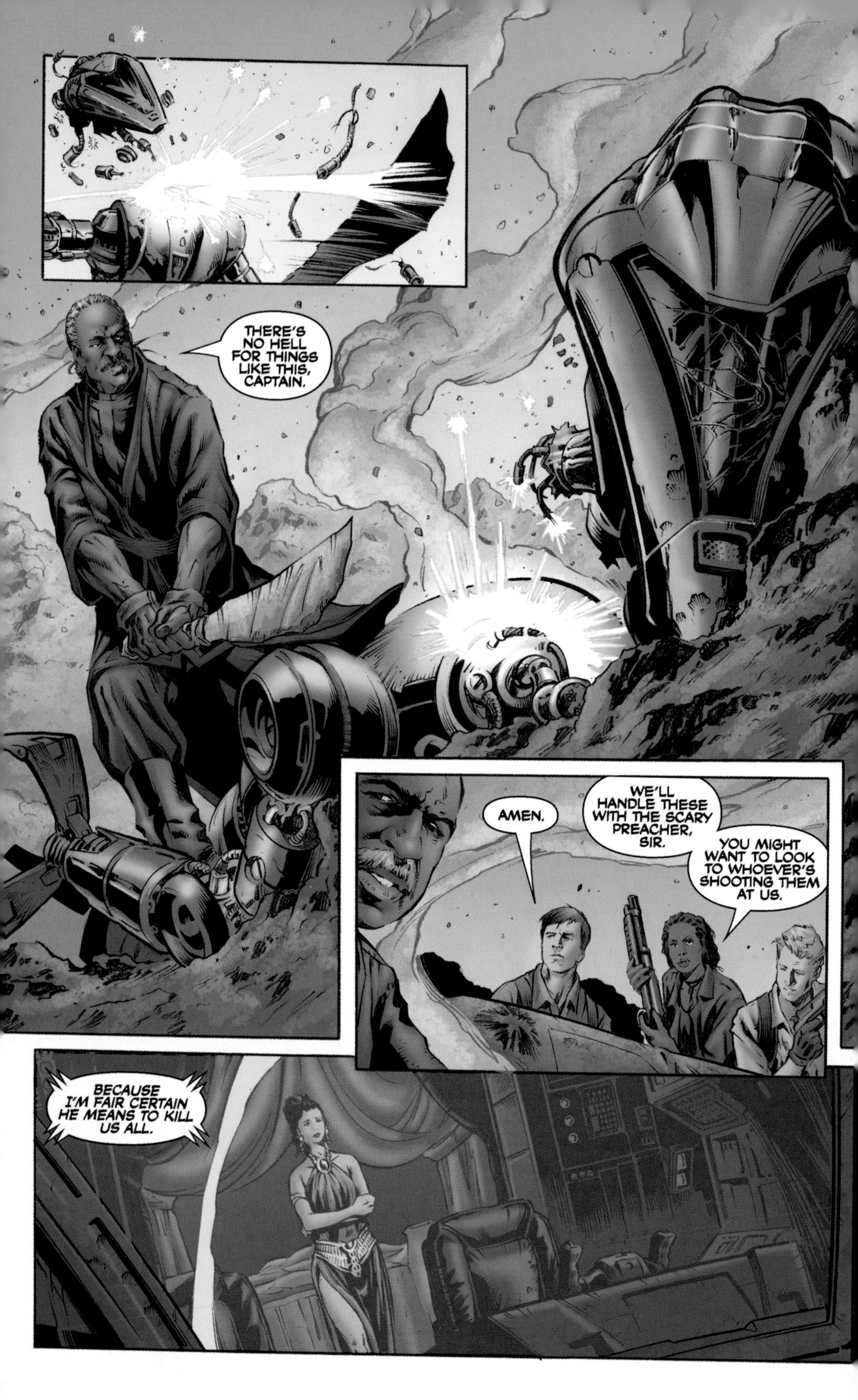
THERE'S NO HELL FOR THINGS LIKE THIS, CAPTAIN.
AMEN.
WE'LL HANDLE THESE WITH THE SCARY PREACHER, SIR.
YOU MIGHT WANT TO LOOK TO WHOEVER'S SHOOTING THEM AT US.
BECAUSE I'M FAIR CERTAIN HE MEANS TO KILL US ALL.

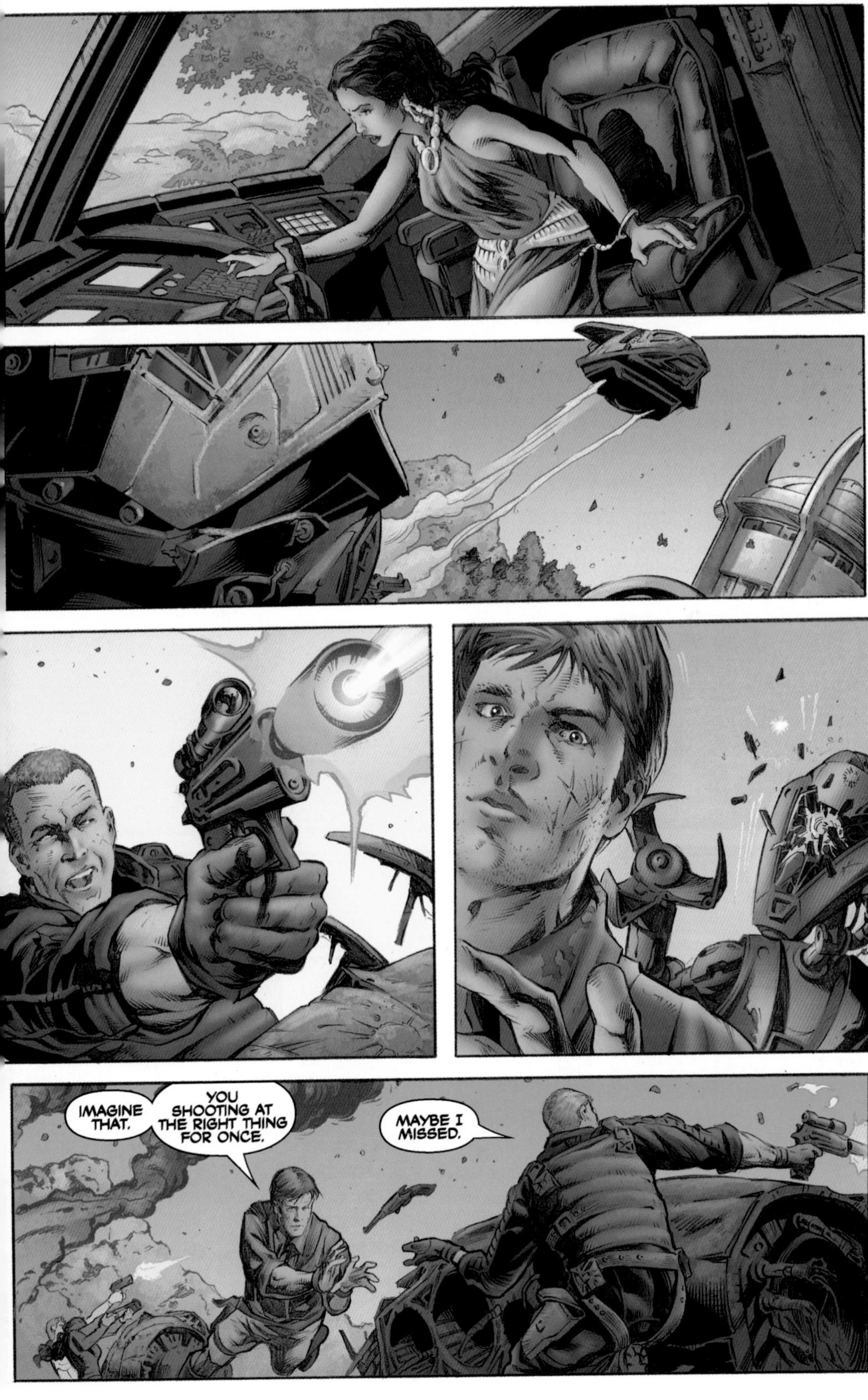
IMAGINE THAT.
YOU SHOOTING AT THE RIGHT THING FOR ONCE.
MAYBE I MISSED.

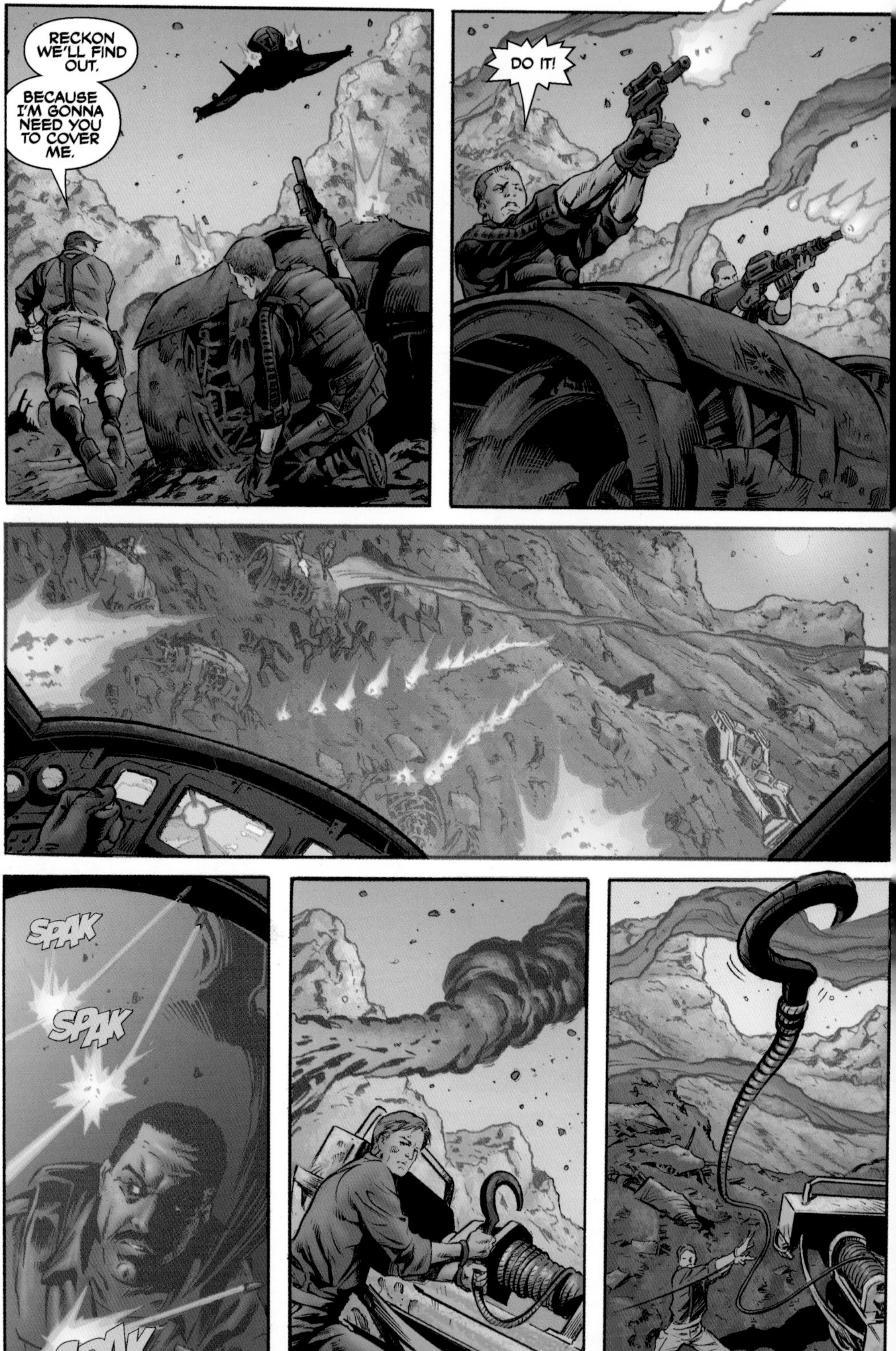
RECKON WE'LL FIND OUT.
BECAUSE I'M GONNA NEED YOU TO COVER ME.
DO IT!
SPAK
SPAK
SPAK

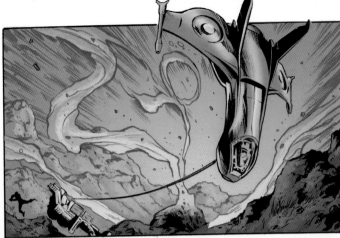

GUESS WE'LL NEVER KNOW WHAT HIS PROBLEM WAS...

WE GOOD HERE?

GOOD ENOUGH.

ACTUALLY, THERE'S THIS ONE THING...

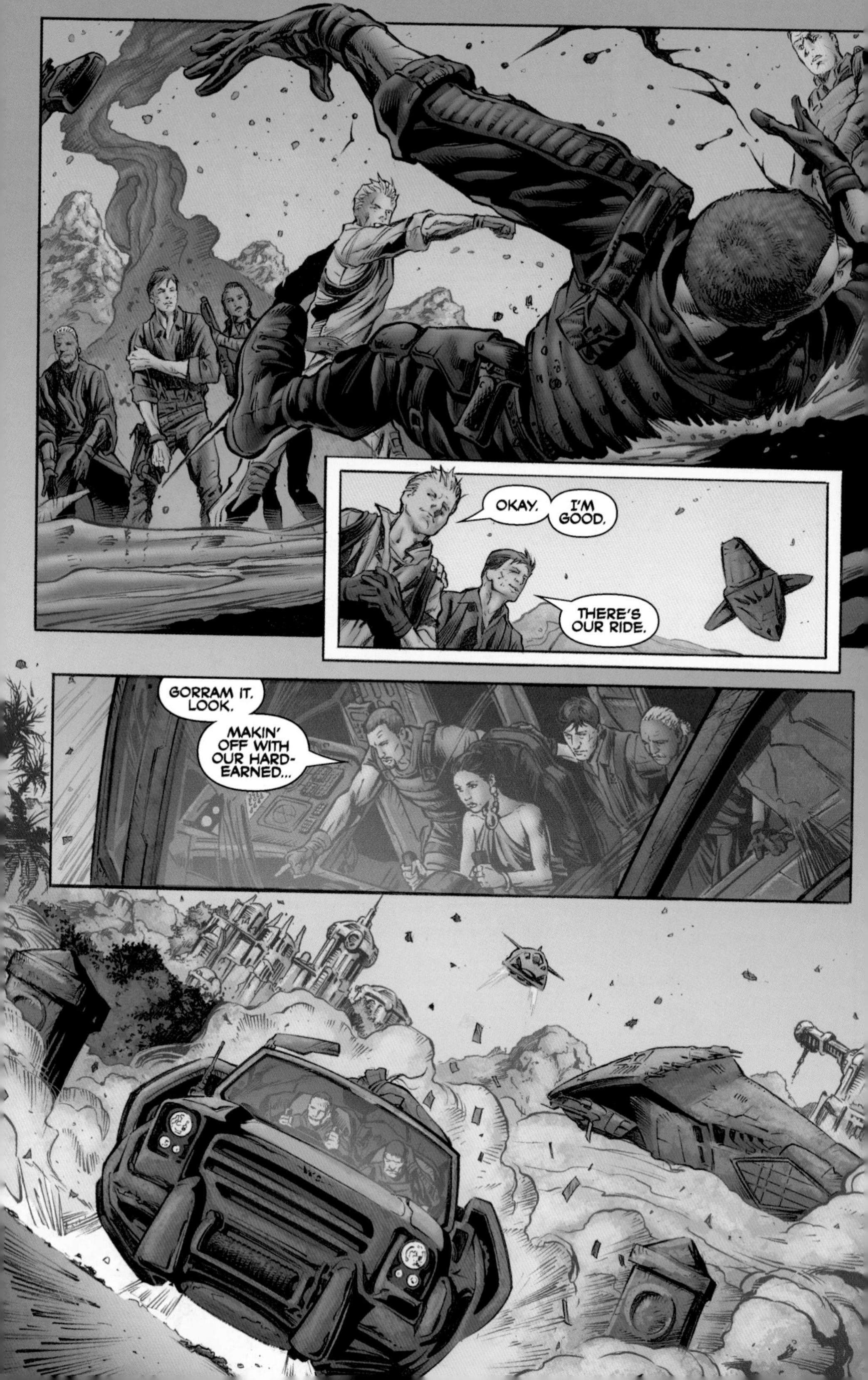
OKAY.
I'M GOOD.
THERE'S OUR RIDE.
GORRAM IT. LOOK.
MAKIN' OFF WITH OUR HARD-EARNED...

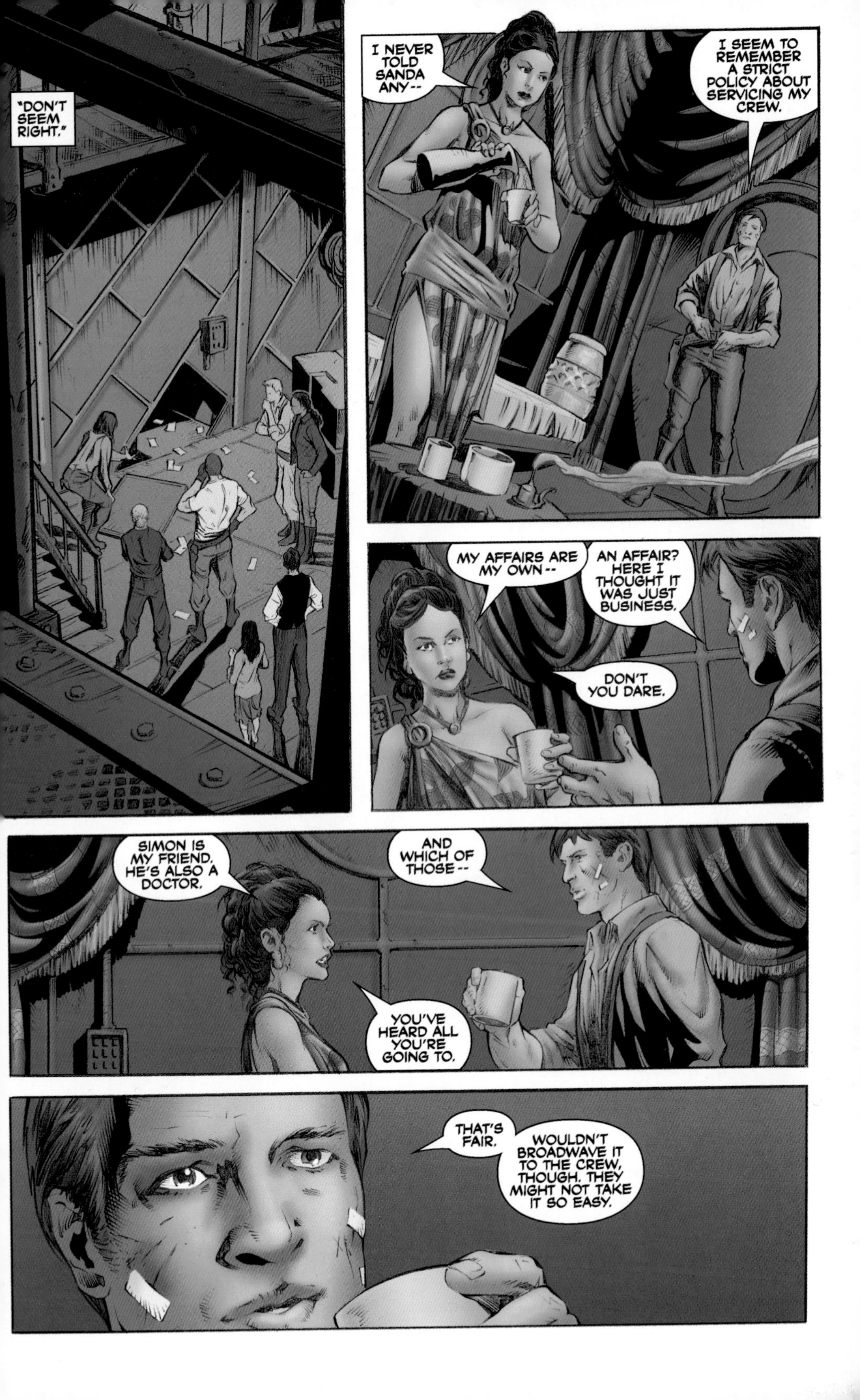
"DON'T SEEM RIGHT."
I NEVER TOLD SANDA ANY--
I SEEM TO REMEMBER A STRICT POLICY ABOUT SERVICING MY CREW.
MY AFFAIRS ARE MY OWN--
AN AFFAIR? HERE I THOUGHT IT WAS JUST BUSINESS.
DON'T YOU DARE.
SIMON IS MY FRIEND. HE'S ALSO A DOCTOR.
AND WHICH OF THOSE--
YOU'VE HEARD ALL YOU'RE GOING TO.
THAT'S FAIR.
WOULDN'T BROADWAVE IT TO THE CREW, THOUGH. THEY MIGHT NOT TAKE IT SO EASY.

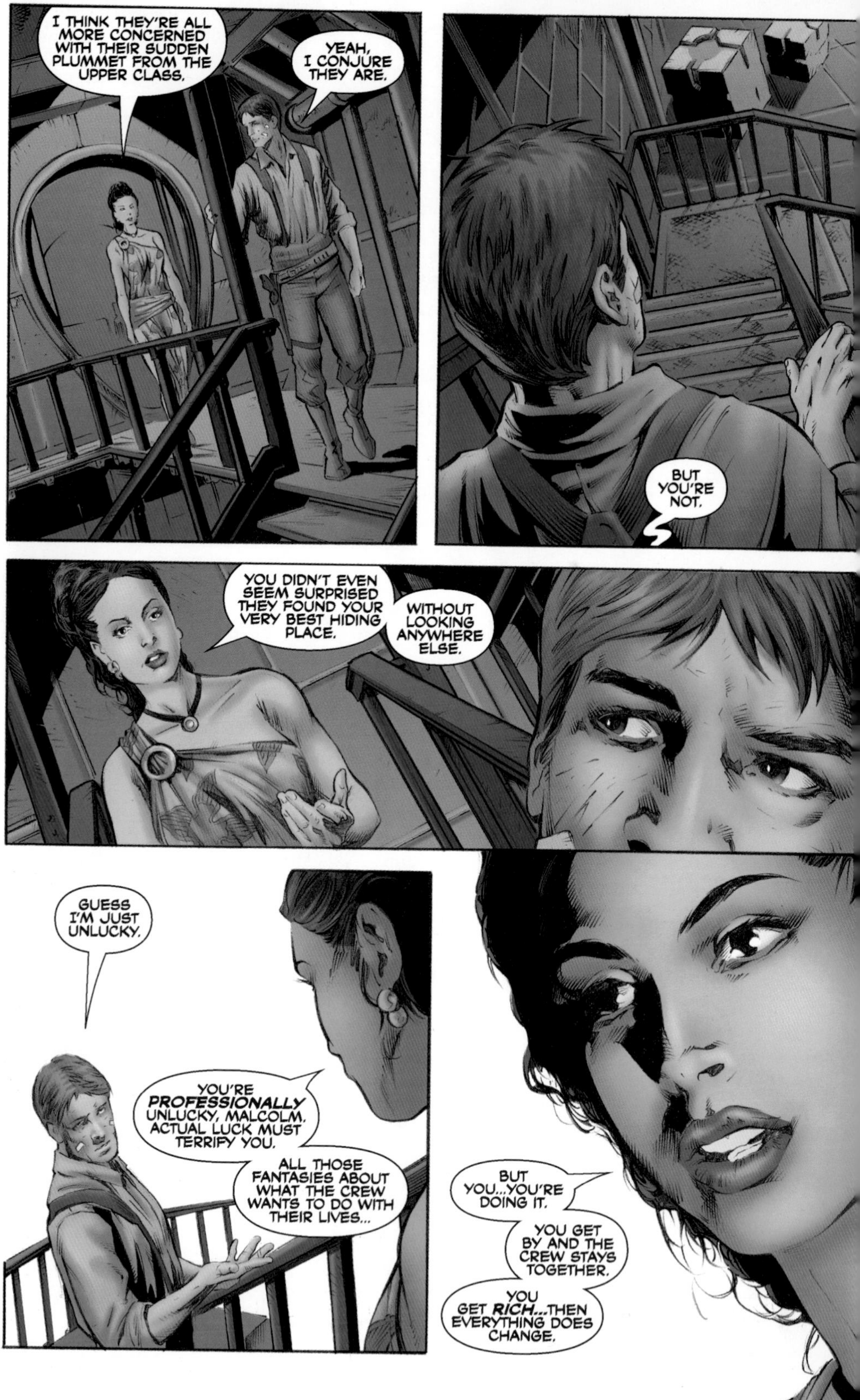
I THINK THEY'RE ALL MORE CONCERNED WITH THEIR SUDDEN PLUMMET FROM THE UPPER CLASS.
YEAH, I CONJURE THEY ARE.
BUT YOU'RE NOT.
YOU DIDN'T EVEN SEEM SURPRISED THEY FOUND YOUR VERY BEST HIDING PLACE.
WITHOUT LOOKING ANYWHERE ELSE.
GUESS I'M JUST UNLUCKY.
YOU'RE **PROFESSIONALLY** UNLUCKY, MALCOLM. ACTUAL LUCK MUST TERRIFY YOU.
ALL THOSE FANTASIES ABOUT WHAT THE CREW WANTS TO DO WITH THEIR LIVES...
BUT YOU...YOU'RE DOING IT.
YOU GET BY AND THE CREW STAYS TOGETHER.
YOU GET **RICH...**THEN EVERYTHING DOES CHANGE.

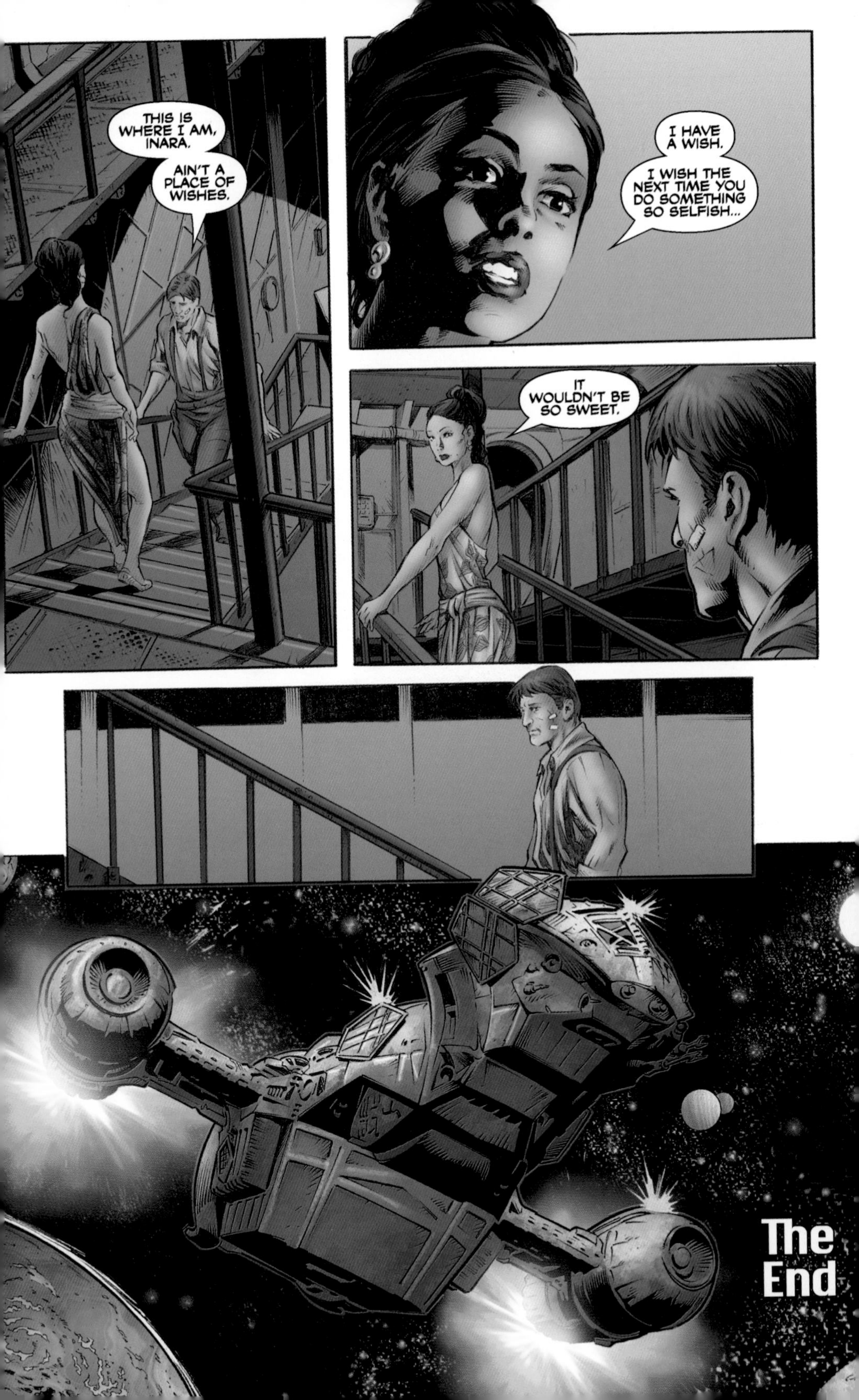
THIS IS WHERE I AM, INARA.
AIN'T A PLACE OF WISHES.
I HAVE A WISH.
I WISH THE NEXT TIME YOU DO SOMETHING SO SELFISH...
IT WOULDN'T BE SO SWEET.
The End

ALSO FROM JOSS WHEDON

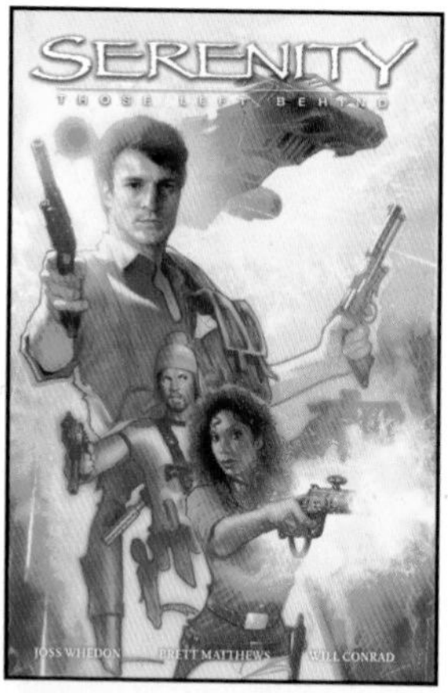
SERENITY
THOSE LEFT BEHIND
JOSS WHEDON
BRETT MATTHEWS
WILL CONRAD

SERENITY: THOSE LEFT BEHIND HC

Joss Whedon, Brett Matthews, Will Conrad, and Adam Hughes

Joss Whedon, the pop-culture mastermind behind *Buffy the Vampire Slayer*, bridged the gap between his cult-hit *Firefly* TV series and his Serenity motion picture with this three-issue miniseries. Sporting a new cover by Adam Hughes, this oversized collection features an array of pinups by phenomenal guest artists. In addition, over a dozen back up pages provide behind the scenes-original material assembled especially for this hardcover edition.

ISBN: 978-1-59307-846-1
$19.95

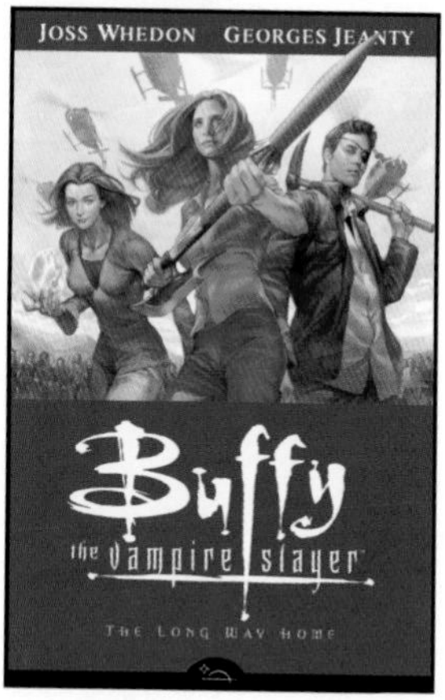
JOSS WHEDON GEORGES JEANTY
Buffy
the vampire slayer
THE LONG WAY HOME

BUFFY THE VAMPIRE SLAYER: THE LONG WAY HOME

Joss Whedon, Georges Jeanty, Jo Chen, and Paul Lee

Since the destruction of the Hellmouth, the Slayers—newly legion—have gotten organized and are kicking some serious undead butt. But not everything's fun and firearms, as an old enemy reappears and Dawn experiences some serious growing pains. *Buffy* creator Joss Whedon brings *Buffy* back to Dark Horse in this direct follow-up to Season Seven of the smash-hit TV series.

ISBN: 978-1-59307-822-5
$15.95

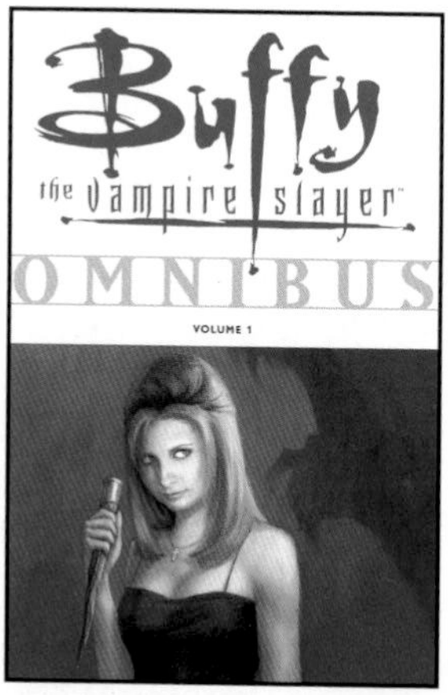
Buffy
the vampire slayer
OMNIBUS
VOLUME 1

BUFFY THE VAMPIRE SLAYER OMNIBUS, VOLUME 1

The definitive comics collection of all things *Buffy* starts here. This first massive volume begins at the beginning—*The Origin*, a faithful adaptation of creator Joss Whedon's original screenplay for the film that started it all—and leads into the first season of *Buffy the Vampire Slayer* television series.

ISBN: 978-1-59307-784-6
$24.95

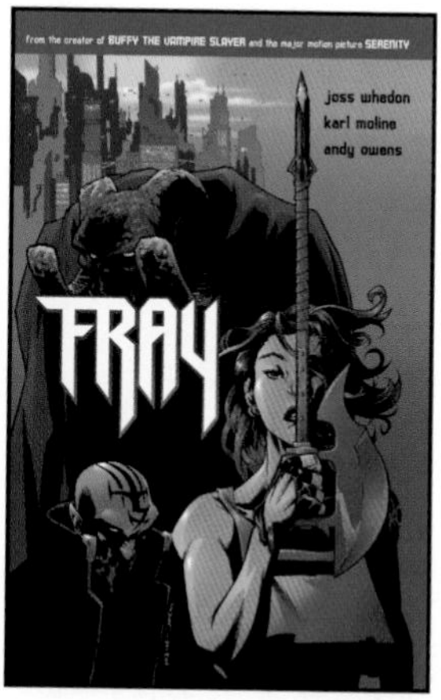
joss whedon
karl moline
andy owens
FRAY

FRAY

Joss Whedon, Karl Moline, and Andy Owens

In a future Manhattan so poisoned it doesn't notice the monsters on its streets, it's up to a gutter-punk named Fray to unite a fallen city against a demonic plot to consume mankind. But will this girl who thought she had no future embrace her destiny—as the first vampire Slayer in centuries—in time?

ISBN: 978-1-56971-751-6
$19.95